Young Writers 2005 POETRY COMPETITION

Playground Poets

Let your creativity flow...

GW00724620

- Pint-Sized Poets Vol I
Edited by Donna Samworth

 Young**Writers**

First published in Great Britain in 2006 by:
Young Writers
Remus House
Coltsfoot Drive
Peterborough
PE2 9JX
Telephone: 01733 890066
Website: www.youngwriters.co.uk

SB ISBN 1 84602 394 7

Foreword

Young Writers was established in 1991 and has been passionately devoted to the promotion of reading and writing in children and young adults ever since. The quest continues today. Young Writers remains as committed to the fostering of burgeoning poetic and literary talent as ever.

This year's Young Writers competition has proven as vibrant and dynamic as ever and we are delighted to present a showcase of the best poetry from across the UK. Each poem has been carefully selected from a wealth of *Playground Poets* entries before ultimately being published in this, our thirteenth primary school poetry series.

Once again, we have been supremely impressed by the overall high quality of the entries we have received. The imagination, energy and creativity which has gone into each young writer's entry made choosing the best poems a challenging and often difficult but ultimately hugely rewarding task - the general high standard of the work submitted amply vindicating this opportunity to bring their poetry to a larger appreciative audience.

We sincerely hope you are pleased with our final selection and that you will enjoy *Playground Poets - Pint-Sized Poets Vol I* for many years to come.

Contents

Park Lane Primary School, Tilehurst

Pelsall Village School, Pelsall

Swailey Gibbons (8)	36
Megan Killian (8)	36
Lee Bond (8)	37
Rachel Dunkley (8)	37
Jade Showell (8)	37
Lewis Cheal (8)	37
Connor Donovan (9)	38
Ryan Mellings (8)	38
Megan Davies (8)	38
Lauren Hubbard (8)	39
Jack Cunningham (8)	39
Liam Fletcher (8)	39
Ruby Sheila Ufton (8)	40
Jade Mansell (8)	40
Jade Hardiman (8)	40
Cody Ranford (8)	41
Stacey Foster (8)	41
Jeremiah Lewis (8)	41
Rebecca Kent (8)	42
Kelly Manley (9)	42
Chris Whitelaw (8)	42
Jack Carroll (8)	43

Pimperne CE VC Primary School, Pimperne

Daniel Buckley (8)	43
Andrew Smith (8)	43
Christian Flavell (9)	44
James Willis-Fisher (8)	44
Jamie Howarth (8)	44
Ursula Sheldrake (8)	45
Harry Owen (8)	45
Amy Oliver (9)	45
Cameron Corfield (8)	46
Georgina Martin (8)	46
Freya Edwards (8)	46
James Bethell (8)	47
Amy Gill (8)	47
Rhiannon Donohoe (8)	47

Ravenstonedale Endowed Primary School, Ravenstonedale

St Aldhelm's CE VA Combined School, Branksome

St Dunstan's Catholic Primary School, Woking

Harry Smith (10)	68
James Tilley (8)	68
Rosie Murphy (11)	69
Ailsa Grigsby (8)	69
Katherine Clifton (10)	70
Jake O'Leary (8)	70
Levi Vassell (8)	71
Alexandra Ranford (8)	71
Isabel Scadeng (10)	72
Luke Perera (9)	72
Andrew Fenning (11)	73
Anna Phillips (8)	73
Grace Sinclair (10)	74
Luca Gilfillan (8)	74
Sophie Fidge (10)	75
Emily Blayney (8)	75
Jamie McNicholas (8)	76
Georgina Halls (8)	76
Mark Harvey (9)	77
Louis Wellbelove (9)	77
Aaran Carr (10)	78
Jack Chisholm (8)	78
Tommy Lawlor (11)	79
Jordan Lee (8)	79
Jade Currie (11)	80
Alex Ingram (10)	80
Connor Spruzs (10)	81
Lucia Caruso (11)	81
Emily Woods (10)	82
Shauna Lopez (11)	82
Louise Bittleston (10)	83
Matthew Stedman (10)	83
Hannah Harvey (11)	84
Harry Blackmore (10)	84
Laura Cox (10)	85
Gabriella Scognamiglio (10)	85
Oriana Malvasi (10)	86
Robert Fletcher (10)	86
Anna Rhodes (11)	87

St Helen's Primary School, Condorrat

Daniel Hansen (9)	87
Louis Feighan (9)	88
Joseph Quinn-Toye (10)	88
Lisa Agyako (10)	89
Joanne O'Neill (10)	90
Katie O'Connor (10)	91
Hannah Moore (10)	92
Mark Kennedy (10)	93
Farran Smith (10)	94
Caitlin Rennie (10)	95
Claire Haughey (10)	96
Sophie Gilbride (9)	97
Chloe Shields (10)	98
Emma McColl (10)	99
Caitlin Divers (10)	100
Juliette Carson	101

St Jarlath's Primary School, Blackwatertown

Charlie McGleenan (10)	102
Bradley Dynes (10)	102
Shannen Hughes (11)	103
Anthony Mackle (11)	103
Tony Doherty (11)	104
Nayana Mary Saju (12)	104
Aoife McKenna (10)	105
Louise Donnelly (10)	105
Emma Rafferty (10)	106
Ryan Hughes (10)	106
Laura Finn (11)	107
Liam McKenna (10)	107
Chloe Starkey (11)	108
Niamh McElroy (11)	109
Michelle Graham (11)	110

St Mark's Elm Tree CE VA Primary School, Fairfield

Hero Gough (7)	110
Anna Levin (8)	111
William Noble (7)	111
Chloe Hooker (7)	112

St Mary's Primary School, Bonnyrigg

Siobhan Turnbull (7)	124
Liam Lothian (8)	124
Beatrice Begg (8)	125
Glenn Wood (8)	125
Mattia Emiliana Ocone (7)	125
Aaron Milne (8)	125
Sean Cocker (7)	126
Nicole Rutherford (8)	126
Hailey McCulloch (7)	126
Matthew Graham (8)	127
T J Connell (8)	127
Darren McBay (8)	127

SS Wulstan's & Edmund's Catholic Primary School & Nursery, Fleetwood

Alice Urwin (10)	128
Megan Bennett-Tipping (10)	128
Connor McGladdery (10)	129
Conor Kaye (10)	130
Jack Conneely (10)	130
Faye Simpson (10)	131
Thomas Greenall (9)	131
Lucinda Denney (10)	132
Chloe Atkinson (10)	132
Jenny Mottershead (9)	133
Emily Brand (9)	133
Chloe McLaughlin (10)	134
Olivia Darbyshire (10)	134
James Delaney (9)	135
Jamie Greenall (10)	135
Faye Eardley	135
Libby Tegan Ramsbottom (11)	136
Sophie Shields (10)	136
Amy Taylor (10)	137
Michael Perry (11)	137
Benedict Tse-Laurence (11)	138
Hayley O'Sullivan (9)	138
Kirsty Graham (10)	139
Michael Swann (10)	139
Erin Smyth (10	140

Olivia Ikeda-Allen (11)	141
Brandon Garrard (10)	141
Michael Lydon (10)	142
Lauren Wilkinson (9)	142
Louise Ward (10)	142
Bethany Walsh (10)	143
Bradley Mills (9)	143
Ashleigh Blundell (9)	143
Jason Stirzaker (10)	144
Andrew Butler (11)	144
Francesca Warder (10)	144
Louis Robinson (10)	145
Connaire Mulgrew (10)	145
Billy Dollin (9)	145
Lauren Scott	146
Teddi Spearpoint	146
Oliver Cheetham (9)	147
George Benson (9)	147
Sammy Drury (11)	147
Summer Bailey	148
Connor Benson (10)	148

Sherington Primary School, Charlton

Paige Rogers & Lewis Wilson (8)	148
Rebecca Terry (8)	149
China Ryan (9)	149
Paris Tomlinson (9)	150
Tolu Olamiyam (8)	150
Wilhem J Ngaka (8)	150
Cameron Hand (9)	151
Grant Biddiss (8)	151
Chloe Hearnden (8)	151
Melissa Barden (9)	152
Tyler Bruiners (8)	152
Ellie Deverill (8)	153

Skelton Newby Hall CE School, Ripon

Anna Louise Moore (10)	153
Imogen Hughes (9)	154
Sophie Dumbreck (9)	154
Jack Sheridan (8) & Thomas Chappell (7)	155

The Heys Primary School, Ashton-under-Lyne

Uplands CP School, Stroud

Wilburton VPC School, Ely

Melissa Blundell (9)	172
Bethany Flack (10)	173
Freddie Upton (9)	173
Jenny Weldon (11)	174
Joshua Robinson (10)	174
Anjela Griffiths (11)	174
Christopher Coe (9)	175
Harley Pyne (10)	175
Abigail Weldon (9)	175
Jade Harris (9)	176
Philip Kirby (10)	176
Brook Line (9)	176
Austin Line (10)	177
Josh Greene (10)	177
Katie Easton (10)	178
Ryan Dodd (10)	178
Ross Payne (10)	178
Mellissa Binks (10)	179

Ysgol Cynfran, Colwyn Bay

Anna Fletcher (10)	179
Brian Williams (10)	180
Immogen Steward (9)	180
Jemma Roberts (9)	181
Jessica Foster (9)	181
Sam Faux (9)	182
Ashleigh Jordan Howard	182
Dillon James Faux (9)	182
Caen Warren (10)	183
India Hughes (9)	183
Rhys Rowlings	184
Leila Parker (9)	184
John Mark Gill (9)	185

The Poems

The Magic Box (My Favourite Things)

(Based on 'Magic Box' by Kit Wright)

I will put into the box . . .
The lively lily from the long garden,
The teeth from a torturing T-rex,
The swift sky shifting high above.

I will put into the box . . .
The greenest tree of the greenest forest,
The yell of a quiet child,
The sweetest sip from the Queen's fountain.

I will put into the box . . .
The laughter of children in the playground,
The first kiss from my mum,
The last laugh from my body.

I will put into the box . . .
Ice-cold fire and burning ice,
A harmless great white shark
And a killer salmon.

My box is fashioned from . . .
Pure non-melting gold and silver,
A lock that only takes the perfect key
And the hinges are only joined by love.

I shall snowboard in my box,
Performing the best tricks and stunts ever made
And I shall land on a comfortable bed of feathers
I will be the best duellist in the history of Yu-Gi-Oh
And I will have fun with all my best friends.

Myles L Grayson (10)

The River Poem

The river . . .
Speeding
Wrinkly
Rough
Racing
Rocky
Swirling.

Alan Heywood (8)
Manor Primary School, Ivybridge

Loneliness

Loneliness means you've no one to talk to when you're hurt
or upset.
Loneliness means you've no one to bring you inside out of
the cold or the wet.

Loneliness means nobody loves you.
Loneliness means nobody cares.
Loneliness means you're all by yourself because no one else
wants to be there.

Loneliness means you've no one to chat to about the news
or your new mobile phone.
Loneliness means nobody listens when you start to moan.

Loneliness means no one says hello or goodbye.
Loneliness means no one gives sympathy when you cry.

So next time you say that you're lonely, it might be time to stop
and think.
Some people out there have no one, like a boat that's ready to sink.

Jessie Smith (10)
Nether Green Junior School, Sheffield

Bonfire Night

On Bonfire Night you can hear lots of different noises,
You look out the window and see loads of colourful fireworks,
Bursting and flying in all directions,
I run as fast as I can to get my boots and coat on.

The Catherine wheels fizz and swirl, spinning round and round,
The rockets boom and bang, shooting into the air
And fountains crackle, red, orange and silver.
There are flashes, screams and bright colours from the fireworks.

'Wow!' and 'Aah!' and 'Ooh!' I say,
Children run around screaming with joy,
They write their names in the air with sparklers, laughing,
A Roman candle shoots out fireballs one at a time in
different colours,

The bonfires smoke, flames flicker and sparks fly into the air,
The lightness of the day turns to darkness for the night.
The smell of smoke is in the air,
There are toasted marshmallows, chestnuts and toffee.

The marshmallows go gooey on the inside and crunchy
on the outside,
They smell delicious.
Sticky parkin and toffee apples are fun to eat,
Sometimes you can get more of it round your mouth than in
your tummy!

It is so exciting, I don't even mind the rain!

When I get home I have to get straight into the shower,
I am very muddy!
I wash the smoky smell and the mud off myself.
Clean pyjamas in a clean bed, I crawl in and look out of the window.

I fall fast asleep still watching the fireworks!

Hannah Freeman (9)
Nether Green Junior School, Sheffield

Birthday Thank Yous

Dear Auntie,
Thanks for the jumper,
I really adore the baby-pink.
Now I definitely can't wait for winter.

Dear Sister,
Thank you for the hankies,
I now can't wait to catch flu,
How thoughtful of you.

Dear Gran,
Thank you for the jam,
But after it had been in the post
I picked all the bits of glass out
Before I spread it on my toast.

Dear Cousin,
Thank you for the soap,
I so much liked the pink,
But if somebody slipped on it, just think!

Dear Uncle,
Thanks for the socks,
I really love the luminous orange,
I'll be seen a mile away!

Georgia Haseldine (8)
Nether Green Junior School, Sheffield

The Whale's Tail

In the sunlit waters of the lagoon
the coral starts to burst out in bloom.
The sun rises in the sky,
stingrays buzz, their prey up high.
Across the horizon you can see
the whale's tail swimming away to sea.

Lizzie Rawson (8)
Nether Green Junior School, Sheffield

Loss

Loss is the colour of grey, lonely grief,
which smells of rot and mould,
it tastes like dry, stale bread
and sounds like teardrops' patter.
It feels like a knife through your heart
and casts dark shadows over the world,
it lives down the black hole of death
and travels in the wind.

But through the grey mist of loss
shines the light of hope and joy
and as hope fights off terrible loss,
joy finds its way again.

Clare Carlile (10)
Nether Green Junior School, Sheffield

Seasons

I love summer because it is fun.
I love summer because of the sun.

Autumn is good because of the leaves
apart from all the very bare trees.

Winter is really cold
and it has a breeze.
I feel for the snowman,
he must really freeze.

Spring is when the flowers grow
and baby animals walk so slow.

Phoebe Loates (8)
Nether Green Junior School, Sheffield

Teacher, Teacher

Teacher, teacher, you are clean,
Teacher, teacher, you are mean,
I'd lock you in the cellar,
I'd mess up your hair,
There's nothing stopping her,
She's as mean as a bear.
With her one eye she spies on us,
She gives us a nasty grunt and walks away.
Teacher, teacher, if you are nice,
I'll be nice to you.

Jessica Glossop (9)
Nether Green Junior School, Sheffield

The Universe

His body is the silent, icy blackness of space,
His many heads are the colourful dancing planets,
His eyes are the thousands of twinkling stars,
His muscles and sinews are the magical star constellations,
The heavy stones from his sling are the meteors,
He is a giant, bigger than anything,

The universe!

Imogen Cassels (9)
Nether Green Junior School, Sheffield

Red

Think of something red
A blazing fire is red
The setting sun is red
A strawberry is red
A poppy is red
A rose is red
Red has the darkness of death which is like the colour of blood
How does anyone know what is red?

Ben Renshaw (8)
Newbold Verdon Primary School & Community Centre, Newbold Verdon

Turquoise

Think of something turquoise
The waves in the sea?
A sparkling pebble
Or the sky on a sunny day?

Turquoise is a fish all on its own in the pool
Turquoise is a powerful, strong colour
Turquoise is the waves over the ocean
Turquoise is a calm feeling inside
Turquoise is like the running stream.

What is turquoise?

Siân Yates-Smith (8)
Newbold Verdon Primary School & Community Centre, Newbold Verdon

Purple

Think of something purple
A balloon?
A plum
Or a sari for a queen?

Purple is a rich throne cushion
Purple is blackcurrant
Purple is Vimto.

Purple is the gleam of the stars
Purple is the moonshine.

What is purple?

Bradley Roach (8)
Newbold Verdon Primary School & Community Centre, Newbold Verdon

Red

Think of something red
A sun?
A tongue
Or a fire?

A poppy is red
Blood is red
Death is red
Red has an angry feeling
Red is like an apple about to be eaten.

What is red?

Lewis Gaskell (9)
Newbold Verdon Primary School & Community Centre, Newbold Verdon

Fireworks

F ireworks are colour
I n the air
R eally swirly
E xplode into the hot air
W histle and bang loudly
O ver the moon
R ight up into the sky
K *aboom,* to the stars
S moke burns from the fireworks.

Cerys Statham (7)
Newbold Verdon Primary School & Community Centre, Newbold Verdon

Purple

Think of something purple
A plum?
A rich cushion
Or a sari for a queen?

Purple is happy
Purple is sleepy
Purple is sad
Purple is happiness
Purple is like a rose.

What is purple?

Alice Chapman (8)
Newbold Verdon Primary School & Community Centre, Newbold Verdon

Fireworks

F ireworks go *kaboom!*
I think they're wicked
R ushing through the sky
E xploding where the stars are
W hizzing over the moon
O ver the stars
R oaring through the sky
K abooming till the end
S parkling in the sky.

Cameron Hextall (7)
Newbold Verdon Primary School & Community Centre, Newbold Verdon

Green

Think of something green
The grass?
A leaf
Or cucumber?

Green is an apple
Green is some peas
Green is lettuce
Green has a lot of coldness
Green is like a really cold day.

What is green?

Danny Richards (8)
Newbold Verdon Primary School & Community Centre, Newbold Verdon

Fireworks

F ireworks are loud.
I like fireworks.
R ushing into the sky.
E ven they are colourful.
W ith gunpowder.
O ver the moon.
R ipe red, green, blue, gold, silver and pink.
K *aboom* they go.
S parkles and crackles everywhere in the sky.

Alexander Smith (8)
Newbold Verdon Primary School & Community Centre, Newbold Verdon

Red

Think of something red
A fire?
A school T-shirt
Or an angry face?

Red is an apple
Red is lava
Red is a sparkling hot colour
Red is brightness
Red is like flames that are scorching hot.

What is red?

Ellie Hickinbotham (8)
Newbold Verdon Primary School & Community Centre, Newbold Verdon

Fireworks

F ireworks booming through the sky
I wish I could go up with them
R eaching through the sky
E xploding colourful sprinkles all over the world
W eaving through the stars
O ver the land
R ed, gold, green
K aboom! through the sky
S earching for their land.

Hollie Stanton (7)
Newbold Verdon Primary School & Community Centre, Newbold Verdon

Purple

Think of something purple
A rich throne cushion?
A blackberry
Or a sari for a queen?

Purple is soft
Purple is blackcurrant
Purple is happy
Purple has a flavour
Purple is like a smooth lilac dress.

What is purple?

Zoe Allen (8)
Newbold Verdon Primary School & Community Centre, Newbold Verdon

Fireworks

F ireworks are colourful
I watch them go pop
R ushing through the air
E very Saturday it's nice and bright
W hen the best firework comes on you can laugh
O ver the moon and over the stars
R ed, yellow, green, gold, blue and silver
K ill people but can be so pretty
S moky and hot.

Chloe Martin (7)
Newbold Verdon Primary School & Community Centre, Newbold Verdon

Purple

Think of something purple
A plum?
A rich throne cushion
Or a sari for a queen?

Purple is happy
Purple is grapes
Purple is calm
Purple is crying
Purple is like a book
Purple is as dark as an apple.

What is purple?

Reece Howkins (8)
Newbold Verdon Primary School & Community Centre, Newbold Verdon

Fireworks

F ireworks in the night
I n the air so bright
R eally bright
E verywhere, every colour in the world
W heeeeeee!
O n the run
R eally fast
K aboom!
S o we're all done!

Joe Stephenson (7)
Newbold Verdon Primary School & Community Centre, Newbold Verdon

Black

Think of something black
A bag of coal?
A bucket of soot
Or an unlucky cat?

Black is black mascara
Black is eyelashes on a make-up-filled face
Black is a workman's toolbox
Black is a lot of scariness
Which is like the outline of a pale white ghost.

What is black?

Luke Pettitt (8)
Newbold Verdon Primary School & Community Centre, Newbold Verdon

Fireworks

F ireworks are colourful
I n the night-time sky.
R ushing, swirling, twirling everywhere.
E xploding in mid-air.
W hizzing, whistling through the sky
O n a mid-autumn night.
R ed, gold, blue, yellow, orange and silver.
K *aboom, kaboom!*
S wirling on Bonfire Night.

Michelle Dennis-Hill (7)
Newbold Verdon Primary School & Community Centre, Newbold Verdon

Gold

Think of something gold
A ring?
A bright crown
Or a shiny bike?

Gold is a ring
Gold is a crown
Gold is a dress
Gold has all the glory
Gold is like a rich queen in a golden crown.

What is gold?

Courtney Gell (8)
Newbold Verdon Primary School & Community Centre, Newbold Verdon

Fireworks Night

F ireworks are bright and colourful
I love fireworks
R eally nice to watch
E veryone loves fireworks
W hen they're set off
O nly some people have fireworks
R ed, gold, multicoloured
K *aboom!* in the sky
S wirling into the sky.

Amy Willett (7)
Newbold Verdon Primary School & Community Centre, Newbold Verdon

Red

Think of something red
Magma is red
Fire is red
Our blood is red

Red is the sign of death
Red is sadness
Red is a red pencil pot
Red has all the sadness and is my favourite colour.

What is red?

Rebekah Dyson (8)
Newbold Verdon Primary School & Community Centre, Newbold Verdon

Fireworks Night

F ireworks go *kaboom!*
I think they're really, really nice,
R eally colourful as well,
E ven sparkle in the sky,
W ork really hard on Bonfire Night,
O ver the stars, twinkling and glowing,
R ushing everywhere, place to place,
K *aboooooooooom!*
S o fast, it's multicoloured!

Libby Greer (7)
Newbold Verdon Primary School & Community Centre, Newbold Verdon

Purple

Think of something purple
A plum?
A royal queen's cape
Or a cushion?

Purple is flowers
Purple is a grape
Purple is wine
Purple is joy
Purple is like a rose.

What is purple?

Liam Cole (9)
Newbold Verdon Primary School & Community Centre, Newbold Verdon

Fireworks

F ireworks make me jump when they bang.
I like watching them go like a rocket.
R ed, yellow, blue, green, white.
E xplode and bang in mid-air.
W hizz around the sky.
O ver our houses, over the chimneys.
R ockets blast really high.
K *aboom!* very loud!
S o bright they are!

Damon Hill (7)
Newbold Verdon Primary School & Community Centre, Newbold Verdon

Purple

Think of something purple
A plum?
A rich sari for a Hindu
Or a sky setting?

Purple is a blackberry
Purple is a crystal
Purple is a melting marshmallow
Purple is the power to shine
Purple is like a dark hallway in your mind.

What is purple?

Bethany Swann (9)
Newbold Verdon Primary School & Community Centre, Newbold Verdon

Fireworks

F ireworks are very dangerous.
I think they're beautiful.
R ushing through the sky.
E very time the children choose the fireworks.
W hizz off to the sky at night
O ur fireworks go *bang.*
R ushing over the moon.
K aboom! they go.
S wirling in the sky.

Connor Oakley (7)
Newbold Verdon Primary School & Community Centre, Newbold Verdon

Purple

Think of something purple
A plum?
A rich throne cushion
Or a sari for a queen?

Purple is blackberries
Purple is blackcurrants
Purple is wine
Purple poses a question for everything
Purple is like a bunch of grapes shimmering in a silver bowl.

What is purple?

Elisabeth Russell (8)
Newbold Verdon Primary School & Community Centre, Newbold Verdon

Fireworks

F ireworks explode,
I see them bang at night,
R ushing through dark sky,
E rupting from the grass,
W onderful fireworks,
O ver our heads,
R ed and loads of other colours,
K aboom, kaboom!
S moking fireworks.

Alex Westaby (8)
Newbold Verdon Primary School & Community Centre, Newbold Verdon

Blue

Think of something blue
The sky?
The sea
Or a pair of jeans they are blue?

Blue is pebbles
Blue is ink
Blue is a beanbag
Blue has a bit of happiness in it
Blue is like a chasing wave.

What is blue?

Michael Crampton (8)
Newbold Verdon Primary School & Community Centre, Newbold Verdon

Fireworks

F ireworks go *boom* and *bang,*
I think the sound is very loud,
R ight over my head,
E xploding and rushing into the sky,
W onderful sight,
O h I wish I was one,
R ockets they are,
K *aboom, bang* and *bang!*
S o high they go.

Thomas De Fraja (8)
Newbold Verdon Primary School & Community Centre, Newbold Verdon

Silver

Think of something silver
The tears of a hurt child?
A shining necklace in the wind
Or a diamond ring so bright?

Silver is a strong metal
Silver is an Indian fruit
Silver is a precious jewel
Silver has the delicacy of the gentle flowers
Silver is like a star that catches your eye.

What is silver?

Leona Storey (9)
Newbold Verdon Primary School & Community Centre, Newbold Verdon

Green

Think of something green
The grass?
A pencil
Or peas?

Green is an apple
Green is a whoopee cushion
Green is a pencil pot
Green is happiness
Green is like a dashing river moving down a waterfall.

Stefan Gunbie (8)
Newbold Verdon Primary School & Community Centre, Newbold Verdon

Green

Think of something green
The grass?
A leaf
Or a piece of cucumber?

Green is an apple
Green is some peas
Green is a feeling
Green has all the glory and it is sparkling
Green is like a lovely smooth crystal
Green is a bright or dark colour.

What is green?

Thomas Bennett (8)
Newbold Verdon Primary School & Community Centre, Newbold Verdon

Fireworks

F ireworks crackle,
I n the night they explode,
R eally pretty fireworks,
E verywhere they are,
W histling, whizzing through the sky,
O ver the stars and moon,
R ushing through the sky so bright,
K *aboom,* they go,
S wirling, swishing in mid-air.

Amy Finn (7)
Newbold Verdon Primary School & Community Centre, Newbold Verdon

Blue

Think of something blue.
Why, maybe the sea?
A sari for a special celebration
Or a poisonous berry?

Blue is sadness
Blue is beautiful
Blue is meant to be calm
Blue has all the spotlight
Blue is like a swimming pool, still and relaxing.

What is blue?

Abbie Bradbury (9)
Newbold Verdon Primary School & Community Centre, Newbold Verdon

Fireworks

F ireworks explode in the sky
I think they're great
R ushing up into the sky
E xploding in the air
W here the stars glow
O ver the Earth
R ed, gold, blue, green
K *aboom* they go
S wirling towards the moon.

Ryan Chaletzos (7)
Newbold Verdon Primary School & Community Centre, Newbold Verdon

Red

Think of something red
Some meat?
A dragon
Or a fish?

Red is blood
Red is fire
Red is terror
Red has a bad feeling about it
Red is like an extremely terrifying scene in a movie.

What is red?

Owen Brown (8)
Newbold Verdon Primary School & Community Centre, Newbold Verdon

Blue

Think of something blue
The sky?
The sea
Or a biro?

Blue is water
Blue is a stream
Blue is a school jumper
Blue has the power in a swimming pool
Blue is like the waves in the deep blue sea.

What is blue?

Ashleigh Downer (9)
Newbold Verdon Primary School & Community Centre, Newbold Verdon

Purple

Think of purple
A plum?
A rich quilt
Or a crown for a king?

Purple is a light purple cushion
Purple is a soft and nervous flower
Purple is as happy as the sun
Purple has a calm feeling
Purple is like a quilt born to be worn.

What is purple?

Connor Allen (8)
Newbold Verdon Primary School & Community Centre, Newbold Verdon

Fireworks

F ireworks are colourful
I like fireworks because they are loud
R ushing past the twinkling stars
E veryone likes fireworks
W herever they go they sprinkle in the air
O ver the twinkling stars
R ushing over the very white moon
K *aboom* over the moon
S wishing all night.

Mollie Taylor (7)
Newbold Verdon Primary School & Community Centre, Newbold Verdon

Fireworks

F ireworks go *kaboom!*
I love fireworks,
R ushing in mid-air,
E ven more colourful than anything I have seen,
W ork like a flame,
O ver the sky and over the moon,
R ight and left a firework goes,
K *abooooom!*
S parkles in the sky.

George Warren (7)
Newbold Verdon Primary School & Community Centre, Newbold Verdon

Christmas Time

Christmas time, Christmas time,
celebrate this time of year.
Carol singers, mistletoe,
friends and family, roast dinners, shows.

Christmas time, Christmas time,
celebrate this time of year,
snowman, presents, Christmas trees,
give me extra turkey please.

Christmas time, Christmas time,
celebrate this time of year,
baubles hanging from the Christmas tree,
friends and family hugging me.

Christmas time, Christmas time,
celebrate this time of year,
snowball fights, snowmen too,
get some snow on your shoes.

Bethan Clothier (8)
Park Lane Primary School, Tilehurst

Winter

At last it is winter
The cold has drawn close
Perhaps I should take some medicine
Just a dose.

Sledging in the snow
Is what I do best
Throwing snowballs at my friends
Boy, I'm glad we live in the west

My school concert's gone
Hip hip hooray!
Now I've got no words to learn
Or any parts to play.

Daddy's got the tummy bug
And Mummy's caught the flu
Auntie Lily has a cough
And I can't get off the loo.

But all the birds are starting to sing
And all the plants beginning to grow
Now out of all the frost
The grass begins to show.

But whoa, I say, whoa,
Winter's gone forever it seems
Just another year to wait, just another
Long, tiring year to wait.

Alexandra Miller (9)
Park Lane Primary School, Tilehurst

Global Meanings

Scotland for its
Cold, icy, breezy, long winters.

France for its
Sugary pudding delights.

Italy for its
Round, cheesy, tasty pizzas.

America for its
Boasts about hilarious cartoons, eg, 'The Simpsons'.

Africa for its
Magnificent, patterned animals.

Brazil for its
Highly trained, skilled footballers.

Spain for its
Heated, boiling, suntanned summers.

Australia for its
Opposite worlds to Britain

And England for the
Pleasure of holding this competition this year.

Matthew Penson (10)
Park Lane Primary School, Tilehurst

Untitled

Winter is coming,
The sky is forming,
Snow is falling on the ground
And falling in the city in broad daylight.
The rain is falling down
On fields and on towns.
The bells begin to ring and children sing
And we know it is Christmas time.

Harry Luckcock (9)
Park Lane Primary School, Tilehurst

Winter Poem

Snow is white,
Snowflakes are too,
You can make snowballs,
And it is fun too.

In the winter the windows freeze,
But it's very cold because of the breeze.
When it's hot,
The snow starts to melt,
And Santa goes off
With his black belt.

Ice is cold,
And very hard.
It can wet anything,
Even hard card.

Aqeel Butt (8)
Park Lane Primary School, Tilehurst

Questions

Don't know which way to turn,
So much we have to learn.
Monday morning blues
Which path shall I choose?
Not always about money,
Getting by is just not funny.
Been there, done that,
Bought the T-shirt, bought the hat.
This is all about me,
And what I would like to be.
What it is? I don't know,
But anyway I'll have a go.

Chloe Walsh (10)
Park Lane Primary School, Tilehurst

Snow

Snow covers the ground
You can make a snowman out of it
Ice always comes with snow
It's like they are partners
When it is Christmas
It can snow on that day
Snow is really cold and freezing
It is like a dream come true
It always comes from the sky
Snow is made from water
When it snows and you have a lot
You can have a snowball fight
When it snows you need to wear scarf, gloves and a hat
You even need a coat on.

Megan Lynch (9)
Park Lane Primary School, Tilehurst

The Journey

People laughing and talking,
Birds like feathery eagles gliding by,
The green view of trees, bushes and grass,
As up above the fire burns,
Spitting red, yellow and orange,
The wind nearly takes us over
And up high in the sky we fly,
I see clouds so fluffy they look like enormous snowballs,
Windmill sails whizzing round and round,
Birds singing wonderful songs,
It's different in the sky
Because everything is small down on Earth.

Ellis Fox (10)
Park Lane Primary School, Tilehurst

The Way Spiders Move

The way spiders move
Up
Up
Down
Down
Around
Around
The way spiders move
They scuttle through the hot deserts
And warm rainforests
They make their little webs
And they are warm little beasts
They can live in houses
Rooms
Trees
Leaves and
Bushes.

Callum Tedstone (8)
Park Lane Primary School, Tilehurst

Friends

Friends forever, that's what I say,
If you have a friend don't just use them for a day.
I found a friend, she found me,
Whatever it was, it was meant to be.
When you're upset and feeling down,
A friend will always be around.
A true friend is hard to find,
But just follow your heart and you'll be fine.

Lydia Judd (10)
Park Lane Primary School, Tilehurst

The Space Café

Lodged inside a crater,
There's a Venus venue
With super spacey waiters
And some 'final frontier' menus.
Aliens wait at the door
Till the sign says *open*.
Martians, Earthlings and there's more!
For cosmic cakes they're hopin'
The doors fly open by themselves
A tallish man says, 'Welcome.'
He steps back and he grins
A toothy smile and beckons.

Astronauts leave the sky
To try the comet chips
Aliens call in to try
The crater curry dips
Martians flock at the till
To try the Martian milkshakes
Lunatics refill their turns
With super starlight soufflé.

Jake Clothier (10)
Park Lane Primary School, Tilehurst

Sunshine

S un burns your skin.
U nmistakably hot.
N ever zero degrees.
S hines brightly.
H alf yellow, half orange.
I love sunshine.
N aughtily sends out rays.
E verlasting light.

Melissa Rose Clubley (9)
Park Lane Primary School, Tilehurst

Bored!

I'm bored, help me Lord.
I have nothing to play, such a boring, boring day.
Jimmy's with his nan and so is Suzanne
Bobby's away on holiday, nothing, nothing to play.
So I'm sat here watching TV,
Just the TV, remote and me,
When I wondered *where is Lee?*
So I went and knocked on his door
And he was lying on the bedroom floor.
It turned out he was as bored as me
Finally I'm free.
I'm no longer bored, just ignore me Lord.
Well that's until tomorrow
When I might have to borrow
Lee again . . . or maybe Ben.

Jamie-lee Fletcher (10)
Park Lane Primary School, Tilehurst

The Summer Days

The glistening sun, birds flying high,
Creatures smiling, no one with a sigh,
Children running, playing in the park,
Then the time comes when it gets dark,
But then day comes again,
The sun comes out and the morning's back.
The morning light,
Makes me bright,
You're the afternoon's mate,
I'd find that great,
Then the night-time comes,
I go to sleep.

I wake up to start the great new day,
Then I shout, 'Hip hip hooray!'

Jack Griffiths (11)
Park Lane Primary School, Tilehurst

The Journey

Up, up I go, what shall I see?
I see birds gliding around, black as night,
Aeroplanes zooming by, full of happy people
Going on their holidays.

Up, up I go, what shall I smell?
I smell bacon as sweet as sweet can be
From the barbecues below,
The fire above reminding me of firework night.

Up, up I go, what shall I hear?
I hear people shouting loudly like a lion's roar,
People laughing joyfully.

Up, up I go, what shall I taste?
The taste of the breeze like sugar on my tongue,
Getting lower, my tummy turning, lower and lower.

Lauren Forster (11)
Park Lane Primary School, Tilehurst

Football

F ootball keeps you fit,
O utside in your kit,
O r outside in the rain,
T he points will help you gain,
B y the end of the game the team will have lost or won,
　　　　　　or somebody will have ended up in tears,
A lot of people have enjoyed football over the years,
L ots of people come to watch the match,
L ucky for the goalkeeper who just made a fantastic catch.

David Dunthorne (10)
Park Lane Primary School, Tilehurst

My Teacher Is So Boring

My teacher is so boring,
She is Queen Boring III.
She didn't even notice
When I called her 'Lemon Curd'.

Ms McFawley is so boring,
She never has a laugh.
Her armpits smell, she has BO,
'Cause she never takes a bath.

She talks so very quietly,
So everybody is bored.
I once had so little fun
I very nearly roared.

I think I had a bit more fun
When I caught a deadly flu,
And if I ever had the chance
I'd flush her down the loo.

When there's a replacement teacher,
I jump up and down in joy.
But if he turns out boring,
My friends exclaim, 'Oh boy!'

At the end of the day
There are lots of pickable flowers,
But the teacher is so boring that
She keeps us in for hours.

Brayden Smith (9)
Park Lane Primary School, Tilehurst

Getting Up For School

I get up in the morning
Just when the day is dawning
I yawn later in the morning
Because my maths is so, so boring
I go to play, hip hip hooray
Cos football is my game.
When the whistle blows
I must go
Back to my lesson to start
Is it English or is it art?
We will wait for the teacher to tell us our part.
Before I know it, the day is done
We've had lots and lots of fun
Now the day is done
I walk home, I must not run
In case I fall down on my bum!
I did that once and it was fun.

Lee Parsons (9)
Park Lane Primary School, Tilchurst

Inside the Book

Inside the book is a boxing kangaroo fighting a lion.
Inside the book is a galloping unicorn running around.
Inside the book is a scary gremlin causing mischief.
Inside the book is a crazy skier jumping on a mountain.

Swailey Gibbons (8)
Pelsall Village School, Pelsall

Inside The Book

Inside the book is a crazy frog helping a fish move into its new house.
Inside the book is a beautiful girl disturbing the next-door neighbours.
Inside the book is a lazy man talking in his sleep and putting his
wife's lipstick on.

Megan Killian (8)
Pelsall Village School, Pelsall

Inside The Book

Inside my book is a terrifying storm trooper shooting.
Inside my book is a violent lion roaring.
Inside my book is a friendly cheetah sleeping.
Inside my book is a sloppy dog kissing an elephant.
Inside my book is a loud alligator swimming.

Lee Bond (8)
Pelsall Village School, Pelsall

Inside The Book

Inside the book is a funny dog barking for his mum.
Inside the book is a crazy clown juggling and spinning around.
Inside the book is a pretty princess waiting for her friends to arrive.
Inside the book is an ugly pig grunting for help.

Rachel Dunkley (8)
Pelsall Village School, Pelsall

Inside The Book

Inside the book is a spooky mummy trying to unwrap himself,
Inside the book is a blue fish blubbering for his friends,
Inside the book is a noisy person singing opera,
Inside the book is a mad horse running around the field,
Inside the book is an annoying jack-in-the-box popping up and down.

Jade Showell (8)
Pelsall Village School, Pelsall

Inside The Book

Inside the book is a scary monster trying to unwrap himself madly.
Inside the book is a mad horse banging his head on a hard cave wall.
Inside the book is a mad dog chewing my leg silently.
Inside my book is a pair of teeth trying to bite my fingers off.
Inside my book is a crocodile with big teeth biting people's legs off.

Lewis Cheal (8)
Pelsall Village School, Pelsall

Inside The Book

Inside the book there is an ugly monster trying to give you
    a sloppy kiss.
Inside the book there is a crazy mad monkey singing,
    'We will, we will rock you!'
Inside the book there is a man dressed up as a bear, saying,
    'Can you recognise me?'
Inside the book there is an elephant running around a cage.
Inside the book there is an annoying girl chasing everyone.

Connor Donovan (9)
Pelsall Village School, Pelsall

Inside The Book

Inside the book is a crazy troll dancing creepily.
Inside the book is an ugly ogre hammering a brick wall.
Inside the book is a swinging monkey jumping from tree to tree.
Inside the book is a fighting daddy-long-legs getting ready to have
    a rugby match.
Inside the book is a funny mixed-up clown yelling, 'Help!'
    because he's stuck up a tree.

Ryan Mellings (8)
Pelsall Village School, Pelsall

Inside The Book

Inside the book is an amazing trapeze artist performing.
Inside the book is a cheeky monkey getting into mischief.
Inside the book is a chocolatey bear getting scared because
    someone might eat him.
Inside the book is a lively cheetah running as fast as he can.
Inside the book is a gorgeous princess waiting for
    her handsome prince.

Megan Davies (8)
Pelsall Village School, Pelsall

Inside The Book

Inside the book is an ugly monkey eating smelly bananas.
Inside the book is a tightrope walker walking on the rope.
Inside the book is a witch on her way to a fancy dress party
    with her wicked daughter.
Inside the book is a vexed troll dancing with a pretty queen.
Inside the book is Scooby-Doo running away from a freaky-looking
    monster waiting to gobble him up.

Lauren Hubbard (8)
Pelsall Village School, Pelsall

Inside The Book

Inside the book is a big, fat, three-eyed monster waiting to eat
                              some big, sloppy bubblegum.
Inside the book is a great, big, fat nan eating all the pies.
Inside the box is a big boxer dog waiting to eat a scared cat.
Inside the book is a big hairy teacher called Mrs Foster
                                    waiting to get a haircut.

Jack Cunningham (8)
Pelsall Village School, Pelsall

Inside The Book

Inside the book is a clown tripping over his feet.
Inside the book is a beautiful unicorn tossing and turning
                              her hair left and right.
Inside the book is an ugly ogre looking for his dragon.
Inside the book is a snow queen waiting to make snow.
Inside the book is a skater skating.

Liam Fletcher (8)
Pelsall Village School, Pelsall

Inside The Book

Inside the book is a violent ogre arguing with a skinny old witch.
Inside the book is a cheeky imp getting into mischief.
Inside the book is a fluttering sprite flying crazily.
Inside the book is an evil gremlin spinning and doing cartwheels.
Inside the book is a little devil poking his slaves with his staff.

Ruby Sheila Ufton (8)
Pelsall Village School, Pelsall

Inside The Book

Inside the book a funny clown keeps falling off his unicycle.
Inside the book is the scariest and hungriest monster, eating scraps
                                                out of the dustbin.
Inside the book is a horrid ogre trying to do the splits at gymnastics.
Inside the book awaits a glamorous bride waiting for her future
                                husband so they can get married.
Inside the book is an ugly nan who decided to go to the ball and she
didn't notice the sign which said *Only People Under the Age of Thirty*
                                        and she's ninety-eight!

Jade Mansell (8)
Pelsall Village School, Pelsall

Inside The Book

Inside the book is an intelligent writer writing a book.
Inside the book is a crazy cat singing with a hairbrush.
Inside the book is an amazing dolphin jumping to get some fish.
Inside the book is a lazy fox sleeping by a tree.
Inside the book is a strange dog swimming in a puddle in
                                        the front garden.

Jade Hardiman (8)
Pelsall Village School, Pelsall

Inside The Book

Inside the book is a dopey dolphin trying to jump like all the others
but he can't.
Inside the book is a scary nan putting lots of make-up on
and trying to give the mirror a kiss.
Inside the book is a big fat fish in the ocean and he gets lost.

Cody Ranford (8)
Pelsall Village School, Pelsall

Inside The Book

Inside the book there is a scary tiger chewing her food very fast.
Inside the book there is a very fast lion running to her food.
Inside the book there is a sweet rabbit jumping around outside
the house.
Inside the book there is a scary mummy running around the outside
of the house.
Inside the book there is a scary teacher called Mrs Foster running
around the classroom being silly.

Stacey Foster (8)
Pelsall Village School, Pelsall

Inside The Book

Inside my book there is a green troll; he has sharp teeth
and eats people for lunch.
Inside my book there is a house tumbling down.
Inside my book there is a dragon in a cave.

Jeremiah Lewis (8)
Pelsall Village School, Pelsall

Inside The Book

Inside the book is a pink fairy waiting for his little purple fairy.
Inside the book is a big crazy frog.
Inside the book is a crazy nanny putting someone's pants
on her head.
Inside the book is an ugly dragon waiting for his dinner.
Inside the book is a mum kissing her boyfriend.

Rebecca Kent (8)
Pelsall Village School, Pelsall

Inside The Book

Inside the book is a soft, pink pony galloping around looking
for something.
Inside the book is an ugly ogre hammering a big box.
Inside the book is a friendly, fluffy rabbit in its cage.
Inside the book is a friendly house waiting for his friends.
Inside the book is a scary teacher with a statue.

Kelly Manley (9)
Pelsall Village School, Pelsall

Inside The Book

Inside the book is a scary mummy chewing bubblegum in his cage.
Inside the book is an angry dog killing people with his teeth.
Inside the book is a nasty mom sending people to bed in the morning.
Inside the book is a good, fluffy bunny in his cage waiting for people
to stroke him.
Inside the book is a gorgeous pumpkin looking through the window.

Chris Whitelaw (8)
Pelsall Village School, Pelsall

Inside The Book

Inside the book was a quiet lion sleeping silently.
Inside the book was a green dragon breathing fire.
Inside the book was a quiet mouse creeping around.
Inside the book was a squeaking rat running about.
Inside the book was a spooky person, running to a shop.

Jack Carroll (8)
Pelsall Village School, Pelsall

Fireworks - Cinquain

Fireworks
Make a big bang
Suddenly a rocket
Flies up into the sky and goes
Kaboom!

Daniel Buckley (8)
Pimperne CE VC Primary School, Pimperne

Fireworks - Cinquain

Whizz, boom
It's Bonfire Night
Buying candyfloss, *yum!*
Orange, sizzling, hissing rockets
Goodnight.

Andrew Smith (8)
Pimperne CE VC Primary School, Pimperne

Fireworks - Cinquain

Bonfire
Flying saucer
Whizzing, sizzling, round, round
Crackling, spitting, popping, hissing
Screamers.

Christian Flavell (9)
Pimperne CE VC Primary School, Pimperne

Fireworks - Cinquain

Candy
Is lovely on
Bonfire Night with flying
Fireworks of every colour and -
Kaboom!

James Willis-Fisher (8)
Pimperne CE VC Primary School, Pimperne

Fireworks - Cinquain

Fireworks
Crash, bang, wallop
I'm very, very scared
Boom! Sparks are flying in the sky
Sparklers.

Jamie Howarth (8)
Pimperne CE VC Primary School, Pimperne

Fireworks - Cinquain

Whizz, boom
Up in the air
Fireworks coming now, *wow!*
Round, round, Catherine wheels start turning
Bright eyes.

Ursula Sheldrake (8)
Pimperne CE VC Primary School, Pimperne

Bonfire - Cinquain

Bonfire
Flames in the air
Fireworks in the sky, *bang!*
They were bright, they gave me a fright
Black sky.

Harry Owen (8)
Pimperne CE VC Primary School, Pimperne

Bonfire - Cinquain

Sizzle
The big bonfire
Everyone likes fireworks
The bonfire is very bright, *wow!*
Bang! Bang!

Amy Oliver (9)
Pimperne CE VC Primary School, Pimperne

Fireworks - Cinquain

Fireworks
Catherine wheel
Big crash and a big boom
The fireworks are scary, I cry
Bonfire.

Cameron Corfield (8)
Pimperne CE VC Primary School, Pimperne

Fireworks - Cinquain

Bonfire
Fizz, sizzle, crack
Fireworks roaring, chasing
Red, orange, purple, silver, gold
Sparkles.

Georgina Martin (8)
Pimperne CE VC Primary School, Pimperne

Fireworks - Cinquain

Bonfire
Boom, whizz, pop, bang
Dissolving candyfloss
Catherine wheel turning round, round
Screamers.

Freya Edwards (8)
Pimperne CE VC Primary School, Pimperne

Fireworks - Cinquain

Sizzle
The bonfire burns
Sparklers red and green *pop!*
They were bright, they gave me a fright
Kaboom!

James Bethell (8)
Pimperne CE VC Primary School, Pimperne

Fireworks - Cinquain

Bang! Boom!
Super-duper
Cracking, hissing, popping
Silver bright sparks fizz in the sky
Sizzle.

Amy Gill (8)
Pimperne CE VC Primary School, Pimperne

Bonfire - Cinquain

Bonfire
Fizz, sizzle, crack
Fireworks soaring, crashing
Orange, green, purple, gold, silver
Bang, crash!

Rhiannon Donohoe (8)
Pimperne CE VC Primary School, Pimperne

That's Amazing

Digging the biggest hole
Now that's amazing!

Drinking from the biggest cup
Now that's amazing!

Having a great friend
That's really amazing!

Someone really caring about you
I'd say that's truly amazing!

What about . . .

Winning a hard game?
That's pretty amazing

Seeing your family all together?
I'd say that's quite amazing

Being famous?
That's got to be amazing

Going on a high ride?
That's scarily amazing.

Phoebe Newton (8)
Pimperne CE VC Primary School, Pimperne

Fireworks - Cinquain

Dark night
Fireworks begin
Orange and blue shine bright
Rockets shooting in the night sky
They die.

Emily Thomas (8)
Pimperne CE VC Primary School, Pimperne

Fireworks - Cinquain

Whizz, boom
Bonfire Night comes
Bang go the fireworks here
Zoom here, *zoom* there, round, round they go
Magic!

Ellen Adby (9)
Pimperne CE VC Primary School, Pimperne

Fields Of Green

Fields of green grassy cliffs,
All the summer we like to play,
On top of the hills nothing has a bad whiff.

In the autumn leaves do fall,
But even though they hide in the grass,
We do not mind, not at all.

When autumn goes and winter comes,
The winter season is very cold,
But does not harm the grassy hold.

In the spring grass starts again,
On all of the fields of green,
All of the grass is green again,
No more winter rain.

Although the grass is very nice,
The snow is also too,
But I think the seasons are very happy,
And jump so fast past us like a kangaroo.

Alison Capstick (10)
Ravenstonedale Endowed Primary School, Ravenstonedale

Jellyfish

There's a gigantic jellyfish,
under the sea,
he's big, he's jiggly,
he's a jellyfish, you see,
he's snazzy, he's cool, he's good to see,
he's a big blue jellyfish
who lives in the sea.

Robert Staley (9)
Ravenstonedale Endowed Primary School, Ravenstonedale

War

I can smell smoke drifting through the gaps in the air raid shelter,
I can see my family and neighbours squashed together,
I can hear bombs and planes overhead fighting, killing,
I can almost taste the smoke and fear,
I can feel the damp, cold floor shaking because of the bombs,
I feel unsafe and insecure.
I want to sink through the floor to a distant land with no fighting
and killing,
I want the war to end and all this to stop,
I want to live a normal childhood with fun and games,
But I know I can't.

I am angry, who would do this? Why?
I am scared, what's going to happen? Will I live?
I am worried, what will become of my house?
I am helpless, I can't do anything . . .

It is morning, all is quiet, all is still,
I step out of the shelter and look around,
Houses ruined, streets ruined, shops ruined,
And yet this is not the end . . . it's just the beginning.

Alice Moore (10)
St Aldhelm's CE VA Combined School, Branksome

The Shelter

I wanted to run, I wanted to hide,
But for some reason I was frozen to the spot.
My heart skipped a beat or two whenever the sounds came,
Echoing around like thunder and lightning.

The shelter, a dark and damp cramped space,
I could smell smoke and almost taste gunpowder.
Rats screeching, spiders spinning,
And all that time people were dying.

I was waiting for an all-clear,
But I didn't hear anything.
Just to think, my house gone,
Destroyed along with all my belongings.

It's time, finally the all-clear has arrived.
I rub my eyes, cough a bit, then pause.
My street, gone, only flames remain.
Dust, shrapnel everywhere.

My life will never be the same again.

Tessa Moxley (10)
St Aldhelm's CE VA Combined School, Branksome

Air Raid

I'm cuddled up in the corner of my air raid shelter
It's cold and damp outside
I can hear planes rushing past
Bombs are dropping and houses are falling to the ground
A fire is burning and I can smell the deadly poison of smoke
The sirens are saying that it's not safe to go outside . . .

I wake up and come out of the air raid shelter
My little sister is still inside wondering what's happening
All I can see are smouldering ashes from where my house once was
I have nowhere to stay now, what am I going to do?

George Spicer (10)
St Aldhelm's CE VA Combined School, Branksome

John

It was the day of war, 1st September 1940.
My husband was a member of the Air Raid Precautions.
He sounded the siren. Everyone rushed into their shelters.
I was really glad that he saved a lot of people's lives.
The air raid sirens were still wailing until bombs dropped.
There were . . .
Oil bombs,
Buzz bombs,
Doodlebugs and flying bombs.
My husband was hit by a bomb which exploded and fired everywhere.
I never saw him again.

The air raid sirens, I can still hear.
I remember what happened. I saw it happen.
I will never forget the day.
I was unhappy. Now I have learnt how to get over it,
But I still haven't forgotten about him.
I will never forget the 1st September 1940.
I will never in my whole life forget my husband, John.

I have written it down in my diary,
Which is padlocked and placed on my pillow every day.
I will go to bed and put it under my pillow,
But I will never forget my best beloved husband, John.

Lucy Wellstead (11)
St Aldhelm's CE VA Combined School, Branksome

My Jimmy

It hasn't been the same since Jimmy died.
His uniform hangs in the back of the wardrobe.
The mine didn't have to blow up but it did, under the van
                              carrying my Jimmy home.
Their American voices drifted on the breeze.
But then the explosion, and then silence.
No one could dance better than Jimmy.
We won the 1942 Johnny Boy Cup for 'Best Dance Couple'.
It makes me sad now so I hide it.
He knew all the words to Glenn Miller.
He had the best jive in town.
He was American and had lots of practise.
He parachuted in from a lost plane.
He slipped down the icy roof to the concrete below.
I nursed his broken leg.
It was love at seventeen.
The baby has no father now.
His name is Jimmy, in memory.
The war didn't need to happen, but somehow Hitler made sure
                                                    it did.

Jimmy didn't have to die,
But the Jerries made sure he did.

Elizabeth Harrison Kendrick (10)
St Aldhelm's CE VA Combined School, Branksome

I Went To War . . .

I went to war, me, I went to war.
People died around me, I went to war.
Hitler attacked with German troops,
I went to war, they attacked in big groups.
I went to war, *bang! Bang!*
I felt so sorry for friends that died,
I went to war, my mates got hit in the eye.
I went to war, *bang! Bang!*
I look at army pictures, my team and me,
I'm angry at Hitler, that evil old bee.
I look back at memories that go on and on,
Jerry, Charlie, Jack and Tom.
And now, as me, Mark David, a new and good driver,
But now I think how I was a survivor.

Carlton Moores-Bagshaw (10)
St Aldhelm's CE VA Combined School, Branksome

My Broken Family

My husband was a soldier and got sent off to fight in the war.
That was the worst part of it.
He died as a bomb struck quite close.
We loved each other very much.
Even though I'm proud of him, I still regret letting him go.
I knew he was missing, but I never thought he was dead.
Then three months later, he didn't return.
The next day, my mum told me that my dad and my brother
had also gone.

I cried all day and I wished the war had never even begun.
Everyone that died in World War II will always be in my heart.
I will never forget them, but I hope I can forget the war
And all the destruction it caused.
It broke my heart.

Natalie Wood (10)
St Aldhelm's CE VA Combined School, Branksome

War With Germany

All I can hear is planes flying and shooting over our air raid shelter,
Bombs dropping on houses and trees.
Me, my brother and my mum are huddled up
In one corner of the air raid shelter
Thinking we will never see daylight again.

I am feeling really helpless right now,
Sitting in my shelter, not helping in any kind of way.
I can smell the smoke coming in through the gaps.
My brother is really scared because he thinks we are all going to die.

We hear a bomb drop and the shelter shakes.
We are sitting in the shelter shaking in fear,
Hoping we are all going to live.

Finally we hear the all-clear siren.
I open the air raid shelter door and all I can see is
Loads and loads of piles of rubble and shrapnel.

Lucy Martin (10)
St Aldhelm's CE VA Combined School, Branksome

My Husband Went To War

My husband went to war, so many years ago.
He was a fine young man I'd say,
And he really did love me so.

I had a letter from him halfway through the war,
It caused me heartache,
Like my heart was paper and it tore.

I hated every moment of that silly, stupid war,
There was no point to it,
No point that I saw.

The day of the war, the very last day,
I went to the train station.
My husband's best friend came up to me and said,
'I'm sorry.'

Charlotte King (10)
St Aldhelm's CE VA Combined School, Branksome

The Day My House Was Demolished

It is October 1940 and outside is dark and smelly,
My air raid shelter that I'm in right now is damp and cold.
I can smell fires that are nearby,
Where bombs have dropped and exploded.
I can hear planes flying over the air raid shelter,
Firing at each other and dropping bombs.
I feel scared; my heart is pumping
And I don't know what's going to happen next.
Not only am I scared, my family is also.
We hear sirens telling us not to come out.
Will we survive?

It's morning now and I hear the siren for the all-clear.
There is not much to see or smell now,
Apart from the dampness from the air raid shelter.
I step outside and all is silent.
I feel tired, I have a headache.
Not only is it silent, all you can see is
Piles of bricks and rubble. I can see no sign of my house.
Does it mean . . . ?
Yes! My house has been bombed.
All I have to eat is stew that we made in the air raid shelter,
Unless I find somewhere else to live.
Will that ever happen?

Ryan Fletcher (11)
St Aldhelm's CE VA Combined School, Branksome

That Dreadful, Dreadful Day

It was September, 1940, before that dreadful day,
We were going to get a letter, a letter that would say,
'Dear Mr Greenhill,
You have to go to war,
To serve your Queen and country,
To help to keep the law'.

When I read those few lines on that dreadful, dreadful day,
My heart tore in two and I didn't know what to say.
Why should this happen? Why should this be?
I never did anything to them,
So why do it to me?

One year later from that dreadful, dreadful day,
I got a letter from the army, a letter that did say,
'Dear Mrs Greenhill,
I'm sorry to report,
Your husband died in the war
Where many, many people fought'.

From that day I've grieved,
I've cried all day and night,
Of where my true love may have fought
And where he saw his final fight.

Torin Greenhill (10)
St Aldhelm's CE VA Combined School, Branksome

My Husband

My one true love has gone forever,
Called up into the army.
He went to save the country, I know that is right,
But it is just so unfair, unfair, it is just so unfair.
No choice he has, no choice he has.
Why did he have to go?
I'm ever so proud,
Killing those Germans in the clouds, the clouds, the clouds,
Killing those Germans in the clouds.

Then someone came to say,
Three years later,
That he has gone, has gone, has gone, he has gone.
Thanks to the Germans, the one I'll never forget,
Has gone, has gone, you bet, you bet.
How will I live all alone in the world?
My husband has gone to a better place,
No war, no bad things, he will be all right, I hope,
But now I'm left broken-hearted.

Chloe Braddock (10)
St Aldhelm's CE VA Combined School, Branksome

The Photo

I keep a photo under my bed,
A photo of my son,
With teeth so white, lips ruby-red,
How I hate those awful guns.

I keep a photo under my bed,
It often makes me cry.
They shot him down, they ran away
And left him there to die.

I keep a photo under my bed,
Why did I let him go?
There's no one left for me to love,
Oh how I miss him so.

Summer-Louise Baksa (10)
St Aldhelm's CE VA Combined School, Branksome

A Miserable Night

It was a dark, foggy night
and all I could hear in the shelter
was the bombs of German planes
raging into the distance.

All I could do was sit there,
huddled up in the corner of the air raid shelter,
waiting for the siren,
for the all-clear.

I couldn't sleep that night, waiting to die,
waiting to leave the Earth.
Next morning I came out of the air raid shelter
and looked at my house.
All I could see was black smoke, fire raging
in the rubble of our house.

When I saw the house I cried
to the very end of World War II.

Jacob Smith (10)
St Aldhelm's CE VA Combined School, Branksome

The War

66 years ago today, something terrible happened,
The second time a war broke out.
It seemed like it would never end.

'It will all be over by Christmas,' they used to say.
Times that by five, of course, and add a day.

On every birthday we saved up coupons,
And for icing, cardboard painted white.
Oh how it tasted horrible every time you took a bite.

Everybody killing each other,
Why can't they just toss a coin?

You may now see how hard it is not knowing
What's going to happen the next day.

Amy Macmillan (11)
St Aldhelm's CE VA Combined School, Branksome

The Night Demolition

It is a dark and scary night,
You can't see a thing,
Planes are gliding past
And smoke is seeping round.
Smells of flames that are burning,
I am afraid, shocked and worried.

Will I ever wake up, or will this be the end?
Only time will tell.

I am trying to get some sleep,
Not even knowing what's happening.
Bangs and *crashes* are sounding,
Flames are roaring.
I can hear babies wailing and footsteps running.
I am hoping my family and friends are safe.

I am very disturbed with the goings on.
Guns *bang!* Sirens *wail.*
The shelter is misty, smelly, cold and damp,
But at last I fall asleep.

The morning sun dawns,
I finally awake, outside is dusty and still.
The ruins of houses just two streets away,
The smell of smoke, dust, gunpowder and fire fills the air . . .

I look towards my house and all that is there
Is smouldering rubble.
All my possessions are gone, gone!
I am horrified at what has happened.
All that is there in the sizzling heap
Is my tattered teddy bear.

Ben Carter (11)
St Aldhelm's CE VA Combined School, Branksome

The Morning In October 1940

The siren keeps sounding aloud.
Everyone rushes to get into their air raid shelters.
You tumble out of bed, yet to face
The cold night breeze on your bare face.

You are trying to get to sleep but it's impossible,
The sirens will not be quiet.
Eventually you get to sleep, it's a light sleep though.
You are struggling to get to sleep with the bombs, bangs and sirens.

You are dreaming a dream.
You are playing with your family in the local field.
It's all fine, then a bomb drops in your dream,
It turns into a nightmare.

You are asleep, but you can still feel the ground vibrating
And hear shrapnel dropping.
You wake up, a big bang has just sounded,
The biggest bang of the night.
Finally, dawn breaks.

You go outside, relieved it's all over for today and you're alive.
Even though it's a dull day, with all the toxic smoke in the air,
It seems very bright to you, after being in
The pitch-black shelter all night.

Finally your sight clears, you turn around, your house is gone.
In its place there is a ruin with smoke coming off of it.
All you can see are odd items that have survived the bomb.
Where will you go to now?
The facts of war, so painful to the heart.
Why the cruelty and killing and destroying?

Bethany Tutton (11)
St Aldhelm's CE VA Combined School, Branksome

In The Night Shelter

I'm sitting here in the air raid shelter.
All I can hear are planes flying and bombs dropping.
I'm scared and worried,
I don't know what's happening.
Will the war ever end?

We hear a bang,
The shelter shakes,
We huddle together,
I'm really scared,
I can smell smoke
And feel heat.
Will I survive?

The smell gets stronger,
The heat gets hotter,
The all-clear siren goes.
I step out of the shelter
And look to where my house once stood,
But all I see is a pile of bricks.

Claudia Hill (10)
St Aldhelm's CE VA Combined School, Branksome

60 Years On

60 years on and I hear the screams, the guns, the echoes.
I wish I'd never joined up!

They lay there dead, ghostly white,
I wish I'd never joined up!

I weep at the memories, the screams, the guns, the dead.
I wish I'd never joined up!

We will remember them.

Elizabeth Cull (10)
St Aldhelm's CE VA Combined School, Branksome

Inside An Air Raid Shelter

It's dark, you can't see a thing.
You can't tell if bombs will drop.
Hearing the roaring engines of soaring planes,
Wondering, are you going to wake up,
Or will you ever see daylight again?

Will it be the last time you will ever see your house,
Or when you get out, will you see your house standing?
It's pitch-black, you are cold and confused.
You feel so helpless, you can't do a thing to help.

Crouched in the corner,
You can smell smoke everywhere,
All you can hear are bombs,
Houses getting destroyed all night long,
Great memories are getting destroyed.
Wondering if you will ever see daylight again.

Aaron Golding (11)
St Aldhelm's CE VA Combined School, Branksome

He Said He'd Never Fight

He said he'd never fight and I thought that was true
Because he would never lie to me or you.
But when the day came, which I'll know forever,
He put on his army suit and left.

We said 'Goodbye' and 'I love you so'.
But then he said to me, 'I'll never fight for as long as I will be.'
Then after that, he walked out of the door,
And me and him were no longer anymore.

This memory is with me for now and evermore,
Because of this war he died,
And my heart died because I loved him more and more.

Hayley Paginton (10)
St Aldhelm's CE VA Combined School, Branksome

I Remember!

I remember when I was young,
I remember when I was in the shelter,
I heard the air raid siren.
I ran into the shelter.
I was scared,
I was alone.
I sat there crying,
I sat there worried,
I didn't like it.
I wanted it to end,
I hated it,
I wanted my family.
I was frozen,
I was anxious,
I just want to forget it.

Danielle Martin (10)
St Aldhelm's CE VA Combined School, Branksome

Friends

If you'd be my friend
I'd break my own leg
And hang it up on a peg
I'd go to school for the rest of my life
I'd cut myself with a knife
I'd read a book for a year
And drink any pint of beer
I'd climb to Heaven
And run to Devon
And laugh without end,
If you'd be my friend!

Samuel Woods (8)
St Dunstan's Catholic Primary School, Woking

Friends

If you'll be my friend
I'll fly into space
And swim a race.

I'll go down a hole
And I'll catch you falling down a big pole.

I'll get you 100 fish
And I'll promise to make a wish.

I'll make a gross eyeball
And sadly fall.

I'll run a race
And taste toothpaste.

I'll stare at the sun
And make a bun.

And smile without end
If you'll be my friend.

Rhea John (8)
St Dunstan's Catholic Primary School, Woking

Friends

I'd go scuba-diving with sharks
Play with darts
I'd bungee jump off the moon
Learn to swim very soon
I'd tidy up the house
Cuddle a mouse
And laugh without end
If you'd only be my friend!

Aisling Straver (9)
St Dunstan's Catholic Primary School, Woking

Friends

If you would be my friend
I'd go to the sun
To heat a bun
Go to space
Without a trace
Climb a tree
Get stung by a bee
Go to school
Sleep in a pool
Drive a car
See Lemar
Eat my leg
Hit my head
Eat a peg
Yell, 'Meg.'
Go to a shark
Say it is dark
Paint myself red
Then call myself Ted.

I would run no end
If you would be my friend.

Gearoid Moore (9)
St Dunstan's Catholic Primary School, Woking

Friends

If you'd be my friend
I'd play football all day
Make something with clay
Eat a bowl full of fruit
Sleep in the boot
I'd punch my brothers in the face
Play with Grace
And smile without end.

Jonathan Cooke (8)
St Dunstan's Catholic Primary School, Woking

Friends

If you'd be my friend
I'd eat thirty mouldy tomatoes
Smell my cheesy toes

I'd climb a tree to Heaven
Or run to dizzy Devon

I'd swim in a green pool
And break a school rule

I'd paint my room purple-pink
And drink black ink

And giggle without end
If you'd be my friend.

Grace Fletcher (9)
St Dunstan's Catholic Primary School, Woking

Friends

If you'd be my friend
I'd hate the Romans for a week
I would live in a sheet.

I would paint the house red
I would never go to bed.

I would skate on ice every day
I'd pay until I stay

I'd play a game of darts
I'd jump in a pond full of sharks

I'd hit myself until the end
If you'd be my friend.

Filippo Carrozzo (8)
St Dunstan's Catholic Primary School, Woking

The Sun

The sun looks like two fiery eyes,
Heating up cherry pies,
Sending heat all over the skies,
That's why the sun is like fiery eyes.

The sun's like a burning rage,
That should be locked in a cage,
It's so hot, it's burning up this page,
That's why the sun's like a burning rage.

The sun sounds like a roaring grown-up,
Who has just thrown up,
In his China teacup
That's why the sun is like a roaring grown-up.

The sun moves slow like a turtle,
Who has just turned purple,
And moans like Moaning Myrtle
That's why the sun moves like a turtle.

The sun feels like a big fire,
Climbing higher and higher,
But it can't burn through wire,
That's why the sun feels like a big fire.

Harry Smith (10)
St Dunstan's Catholic Primary School, Woking

Friends

If you'd be my friend
I'd eat roast every day
Never go out to play
I'll stop watching TV for a week
Kiss a bird on the beak
Play rugby after school
Go racing with a bull
If you'd be my friend.

James Tilley (8)
St Dunstan's Catholic Primary School, Woking

Tree

Above me only sky,
Below me lays the ground,
I stand tall as the morning draws nigh
And sing my peaceful sound.

Across the floor I glide,
With my long arms at my side,
Hear my happy tune
And you shall see me soon.

In the wind my long hair flutters,
Falling to the floor,
A bird or two rests on my shoulders
And hear my song once more.

The rain trickles down my rough skin,
The snow sits on my head,
My fingers as sharp as a pin,
Wintertime I dread.

I watch with droopy eyes,
The clouds run through the skies
And in the wind I blow,
Standing tall in rain and snow.

Rosie Murphy (11)
St Dunstan's Catholic Primary School, Woking

Friends

If you'd be my friend
I would eat mushrooms every day
Play in the snow with no coat
I would stay up all night
Take on a fight
I would climb a tree
Get stung by a bee
And smile without end
If you'd be my friend.

Ailsa Grigsby (8)
St Dunstan's Catholic Primary School, Woking

Storm

I shout and I scream
I am definitely mean
I do have loads of friends
But sometimes it depends
I must calm down a bit!

Lightning is my best mate
He sometimes also hates
The fact we are a bit OTT
We are calm sometimes
But not a lot!

I am always sleeping in the clouds
But when I need to be big and *loud*
I get up, get out and shout!
I look like a dark nightclub,
With lights that flash!

If I hadn't ripped apart,
All those lovely human hearts,
I would not be in a mess,
With this dirty ripped up dress,
For I am a *storm*.

Katherine Clifton (10)
St Dunstan's Catholic Primary School, Woking

Friends

I'd eat broccoli for a week
And look weak,
Get surrounded by mice,
I'd skateboard on ice,
Play a game of rugby;
Make no one ever help me,
I'd paint myself red
And marry Fred.
And laugh without end
If you'd be my friend.

Jake O'Leary (8)
St Dunstan's Catholic Primary School, Woking

Friends

I'll clean my room for a week
I'll play hide-and-seek

I'll fight a snake
I'll dive to the bottom of a lake

I'll eat cabbage for every meal
I'll go out and kill

I'll paint my bed purple with a pen
I'll go in a lion's den

I'll eat rabbit food
I'll get my godmother in a mood

I'll dance
I'll go to the top of the Eiffel Tower in France

And smile to the end
If you'll be my friend.

Levi Vassell (8)
St Dunstan's Catholic Primary School, Woking

Friends

If you'd be my friend
I would swim with sharks in a rotten pool
And I would never go to school
I would ride on a scorpion near its tail
I would jump off a rail near a whale
I would ride a bike up to the sun
I would have no fun
I would climb a tree
I would feed on my knee
'Ring a ring of roses' I'd play
I would trip over a tray
And smile without end
If you'd be my friend.

Alexandra Ranford (8)
St Dunstan's Catholic Primary School, Woking

The Christmas Present

In the deep winter,
Time for Christmas to come,
There's a present inside,
Seeking lots of fun.

He sits there politely,
Waiting some more,
Just crouching there quietly
For the opening door.

Wrapped in blue,
His decorations glow,
He watches the clock tick
To and fro.

The children rush in,
With smiles on their faces,
Hopping around
To all sorts of places.

Isabel Scadeng (10)
St Dunstan's Catholic Primary School, Woking

Friend

If you'd be my friend
I would play a silly game of Quidditch
And eat a bowl of spinach
I would slap my head
And go to bed
I'd dress in brown
And wear a crown
I would paint for a week
And turn into a freak
And smile without end
If you'd be my friend.

Luke Perera (9)
St Dunstan's Catholic Primary School, Woking

Counting Down To Christmas

Christmas is starting,
Summer is departing,
Santa will be coming,
I'm worried about the reindeer,
The turkey dancing in the oven's heat.

My presents will be magical,
They will glow and maybe sparkle,
But don't forget about the birth,
Now that's the thinking bit,
The frostbite snow will be freezing,
But nobody cares at all,
Just remember, don't freeze.

On Christmas Day you dance and cheer,
Just wait until the turkey's here,
It looks big and plump, just like Santa,
The Christmas tree will sparkle,
It looks as big as a building.

Andrew Fenning (11)
St Dunstan's Catholic Primary School, Woking

Friends

If you'd be my friend
I'd kiss a big rat
I'd fly fast on a mat
On my neck I'd wear a huge chain
I'd walk on a running train
I'd jump off a cliff
Then I'd feel stiff
And smile without end
If you'd be my friend.

Anna Phillips (8)
St Dunstan's Catholic Primary School, Woking

Christmas Is Coming

The Christmas tree is standing,
Decorations are waiting,
Ready to be put up for
Christmas.

All the robins are dancing,
The snow and frost are shivering
And are patiently waiting for,
Christmas.

Santa is waiting,
In his grotto in Lapland,
Just snow and snow,
No nice soft sand.

Like a man in war
Stands the tired old snowman
Battling snow
As he stands in his place.

A few presents are wrapped,
Hiding under the Christmas tree,
Waiting to be opened at Christmas.

Grace Sinclair (10)
St Dunstan's Catholic Primary School, Woking

Friends

If you'd be my friend
I'll eat sprouts every day
I'll shout out hooray
I'll live in a lion's cage
Why not in the middle age
I'll stop playing football
I'll stop looking cool
A laugh without end
If you'd be my friend.

Luca Gilfillan (8)
St Dunstan's Catholic Primary School, Woking

Winter

The cold winter has come again,
Everyone has got a glow,
There has been a lot of snow.

Snowy footprints on my floor,
Snow is shivering wanting more,
My yummy Christmas pies,
Singing very high.

The snow is whispering,
I am shivering,
Christmas is here,
It will come again next year.

I am grateful,
My pie is tasteful,
My presents are faithful
I have a sleigh full.

Sophie Fidge (10)
St Dunstan's Catholic Primary School, Woking

Friends

If you'd be my friend
I would run without clothes
Watch lots of scary shows
Scare a tarantula that's huge and scary
Paint myself big and hairy
Stand in a rock pool with lots of crabs
Make myself lots of scabs
Sleep in school for a whole year
Drink a pint of yucky beer
Do lots of dares without end
If you would be my friend.

Emily Blayney (8)
St Dunstan's Catholic Primary School, Woking

Friends

If you'd be my friend
I'd eat a truckload of carrots
Sleep in horses' paddocks
Sit on a baby's potty
Play with Noddy
I'd ride a bike into a pole
I would scream into hot, flaming coal
I'd sit on a sheep
Cry a baby to sleep
Go to bed in the night
Skateboard with no head until I get in a fight
I'd dance around singing nursery rhymes
Shout at repulsive times
I'd jump without end
If you'd be my friend.

Jamie McNicholas (8)
St Dunstan's Catholic Primary School, Woking

Friends

If you'd be my friend
I would eat swede
And I would wear a dress made of seaweed
I would bite my thumb
And I would hit my tum
I would slap my head
And go to bed
I would dress all in brown
And I would nearly drown
I would paint myself black
And hide my head in a sack
I would smile to the end
If you'd be my friend.

Georgina Halls (8)
St Dunstan's Catholic Primary School, Woking

Friend

If you'd be my friend
I would read biology for a year
Eat intestines from a deer
Run around with no clothes
Be in lots and lots of shows
I would go to school for the rest of my life
I would cut myself with a knife
Shoot myself with a tranquilliser gun
Stuff myself with mucky buns
I would die
I would hit my eye
Get polished
Be demolished
Eat some clod
Be Plod (from Noddy)
I would cat without end
If you'd be my friend.

Mark Harvey (9)
St Dunstan's Catholic Primary School, Woking

Friends

If you would be my friend
I'd ride my lunch box on ice
I'd eat a curry with spice
I'd ride a sandwich down a lake
The funny faces I'd make
I'd bomb myself
I'd sit on a shelf
I'd watch Noddy for a week
I'd seek a bear to speak
And laugh to the end.

Louis Wellbelove (9)
St Dunstan's Catholic Primary School, Woking

Fireworks

Fireworks are mad
Never really glad
Waiting at the shop
Ready to go pop.

The prices have been dropped
They really should be bought
Their smiles are going upside down
In their squashed up home.

They are now very excited
There's someone in the shop
They're hoping, yes, they are hoping
They'll hope till they drop.

Yes, they've been bought
They are ready to go popping
But they will have to wait
The lady has gone shopping.

Aaran Carr (10)
St Dunstan's Catholic Primary School, Woking

Friends

If you'd be my friend
I'd put out the sun with a drop of water
Take you to my secret headquarters
Eat my own leg with sauce and scrambled egg
Saw off the head of my friend Greg
Eat frogspawn jelly
With ice cream that tasted of a lizard's belly
Smile without end
If you'd be my friend.

Jack Chisholm (8)
St Dunstan's Catholic Primary School, Woking

Waterfall!

Sprinting down to the finish line,
Water drips through the vines,
Not knowing where it's going,
Animals madly throwing.

It uses courage,
By having some power,
It reaches the finish without some powder,
To pamper himself after a long, long shower.

After it's back to breath,
The others come down like an angry dad,
They all come together,
Water dripping from their leather coats.

Andy won,
But they all deserved a bun,
All the water sprays,
Like a tricky maze.

The next day comes
And they are all in bed like lazy bums.

Tommy Lawlor (11)
St Dunstan's Catholic Primary School, Woking

Friends

If you'd be my friend
I'd eat pepper for my tea
And never watch TV
And never go out to play
I'd throw away all my toys
And never play with boys
And smile without end
If you'd be my friend.

Jordan Lee (8)
St Dunstan's Catholic Primary School, Woking

Christmas Is Here

Christmas is here, it is so jolly,
The holly sings because it is so happy,
The Christmas lights light up and dance round the tree,
The star shines with so much glee.

Santa's reindeer especially Rudolph
Get ready to go into the shivering air
And the duvet covers feel as warm as a snuggly bear,
Getting ready for the excited children to sleep in.

Outside it is so frosty and cold,
The windows chattering with ice on the window sills.

Santa's arrived with all the presents,
Big and small, every size,
Whilst putting them under the Christmas tree,
He's eating all the mince pies,
Putting his feet near the dancing fire.

Jade Currie (11)
St Dunstan's Catholic Primary School, Woking

Christmas Day

Holly pinches in the night
Crackling and scratching on the window
Spike here, spike there
They will never be too fair.

Santa Claus in his grotto
Doing a bit of wrapping
Presents here, presents there
I see presents everywhere.

Christmas trees dancing
Decorations glancing
Trees here, trees there
Trees can never give a glare.

Alex Ingram (10)
St Dunstan's Catholic Primary School, Woking

The Christmas Tree

The Christmas tree is singing,
The jingle bells are ringing,
The trees are on their knees,
Rudolph is about to sneeze.

The trees are decorated,
The people are fascinated,
The people are staring,
The trees are daring.

The people are hearing,
Santa Claus is cheering,
He is on his way,
To start the day.

Mum and Dad are in the house,
Baby crying, there's a mouse,
Gran in bed,
Sister going completely red.

Connor Spruzs (10)
St Dunstan's Catholic Primary School, Woking

The Garden

The trees are dancing in the air,
The sun is glancing everywhere.
The grass is waving,
Saving everything that falls from the trees,
Including all of the bees.
The birds are singing
To everyone right until the day is done,
Which is when the sun goes down,
Giving darkness to the whole town.
In the night,
You can see a wonderful sight,
The night is when the moon comes out,
Shining everywhere without a doubt.

Lucia Caruso (11)
St Dunstan's Catholic Primary School, Woking

Christmas Time

The bells start to sing,
The choirs wrapped up are chiming,
The decorations start dancing,
Because Santa Claus is coming!

The snow is whispering,
Falling and thickening,
The trees partying,
With the birds dancing!

The presents are waiting,
Quiet and start separating,
All being opened,
To reveal sweet surprises.

The children are laughing,
And singing and dancing,
It's Christmas time,
So have some fun!

Emily Woods (10)
St Dunstan's Catholic Primary School, Woking

Christmas

The wind it whistles as it rushes by
Stealing children's hats, they cry
The snow skipping by biting their cheeks
As they play hide-and-seek,
They all sit by
And start to cry
There's so much ice
They need warm rice
With hands like frost
They feel so lost
Although it's cold
They still behold
The joy of Christmas.

Shauna Lopez (11)
St Dunstan's Catholic Primary School, Woking

Sea!

On the beach on a calm day,
I would whisper for you to play,
As I run closer to the shore,
I soak people with a downpour.

People are running on my beach,
While I leap out with a reach,
To catch some fish for my dinner,
The fish run off, but I'm the winner.

People on my beach start to leave,
While I sigh and I heave,
Until I find a nice place to rest,
With no one to be a pest.

In the morning I wake up late,
And search for food to go on my plate,
As I search I see daylight,
The sun is shining, it's very bright.

Louise Bittleston (10)
St Dunstan's Catholic Primary School, Woking

Rudolph The Red-Nose Reindeer

Rudolph dived and leapt through the sky,
Here and there, low and high,
Whispering to the wind as he said,
'I am Rudolph with a red nose on my head.'
The trees waved as he went by,
Soaring through the dark, dim sky,
Here and there, he could hear,
The birds and cats with the Christmas cheer,
The dogs all barked and danced that night,
As Rudolph flew into their sight,
Pulling along Santa's sleigh,
With presents to open on Christmas Day.

Matthew Stedman (10)
St Dunstan's Catholic Primary School, Woking

Sea

I leap and crash onto the shore,
Snapping the boat's oars,
I stare under me, deep down,
All the sea creatures make a town.

I look beneath me,
At my deep blue sea,
I'm surrounded with sand,
Taking up lots of land.

Wrinkly shells lie on my bed,
A sandcastle awaits for me ahead,
Seagulls chatter up in the sky,
They dance around up high.

Strong horses jump and play,
Hitting the water every day,
Children playing with beach balls,
Seagulls screeching, making loud calls.

Hannah Harvey (11)
St Dunstan's Catholic Primary School, Woking

Fireworks

Fireworks are running with anger and with a bang
Some go silently, but I like the ones that go loudly
I found I like the fireworks colour in this dark night sky.

A Catherine wheel goes faster than an athlete's legs
Although they dance like singing pegs
Fireworks, fireworks in the night, burning, burning very bright
They don't know whether to have a fight.

Harry Blackmore (10)
St Dunstan's Catholic Primary School, Woking

Winter Living

Seasons all around the year,
Seasons are always changing moods.
The different seasons are completely different,
In weather, clothing, work and foods.

Winter is hard for
Us all to live in.
Taking us into the cold,
We can't ever win.

Randomly selecting
Its weather for the day,
Snow, ice, sleet or rain
It's extremely hard to say.

The wind throws
Balls of cold
Into the innocent air,
Let winter enfold.

Laura Cox (10)
St Dunstan's Catholic Primary School, Woking

The Firework

The firework flies through the air,
Flying past the dancing trees,
The lightning flashes to the ground in flames.

The firework carries on,
It passes through the wind like noisy children screaming.

The leaves fly round the firework like loud music,
The firework flies very fast,
Then all of a sudden,
It makes a *blast!*

Gabriella Scognamiglio (10)
St Dunstan's Catholic Primary School, Woking

The Sea!

On a hot summer's day,
I gallop with joy,
Getting ready to play,
With my rubber toy,
I wave to the children,
Running back and forth,
I'm really an entertainer, I'm sure.

When the clock strikes noon
They go to eat
And I always know they will be back soon,
So the sun shines down and I relax,
While I warm up my body and feet,
But more and more people come to see
The way I play with them happily.
Unfortunately, the time comes when I start to cry,
But I know they'll be back, so I say bye-bye.

Oriana Malvasi (10)
St Dunstan's Catholic Primary School, Woking

Hurricane

It's a soldier blasting down men with machine gunfire
                                        hard and long;

it's like a turbine, but far too strong,
it sends tornadoes left and right,
it's not about to lose a fight,
tearing trees all around,
I bet you it can hold its ground.
Now it slows,
but the wind still blows,
one sign of offence,
and let the reinforcements commence!
Oh, but look the water level lows -
I wonder when it will come to a close
slowly, slowly, it comes to a halt,
and sends no more bolts.

Robert Fletcher (10)
St Dunstan's Catholic Primary School, Woking

The Volcano

This
volcano's
sometimes shy,
but it's very sweet
and touches the sky,
it can be angry and when
it is, it shoots out lava like
bubbly fizz. Late at night he
goes to bed, in the morning he
wants to be fed, he grabs out at
things, that have tiny wings, burns
them up, never gives up, until he turns
into lava. When he erupts, he sounds like
angry pups, he flows like a stream and when
he's hot he shoots out a beam. There is a path
around the edge, you can walk there until the last
ledge, high at the top there is a nest, that is facing the
far, far west.

Anna Rhodes (11)
St Dunstan's Catholic Primary School, Woking

My Best Friend

My best friend is Joseph Quinn-Toyre,
He is ten and what a number,
Eyes as blue as a moving sea in a hot sun
With hair the colour of wet sand on a beach.

He wears glasses on his wide open eyes,
Gives a bright smile on his face all the time,
When I see him I'm always happy,
Joseph is guaranteed to be someone smart.

His hobbies are football, tennis and netball,
We both play for the same team, Condorrat Football Club,
He is energetic, he is a fast runner,
I feel happy to have Joseph as a friend.

Daniel Hansen (9)
St Helen's Primary School, Condorrat

Badminton

I couldn't believe that I was allowed to go to the badminton class.
Would I be good or would I be bad?

The day came as fast as a rocket going at full speed
I was so excited I thought about it all day
I couldn't do my work.

When the bell rang I thundered out of class
Got changed and ran into the hall
Decided to take a look at the equipment
The shuttlecock was as big as my clock in my room
And the racket was as big as my janitor, so tall.

When we started to play I thought I was quite good at it
When I missed I thought I couldn't do it
But I always remembered, always believe in yourself.

Louis Feighan (9)
St Helen's Primary School, Condorrat

Sport

Sport is great, sport is fun,
You can lunge, jump, hop, skip and run
The crowd all roar when the ball goes in
And I can tell you now it's such a din.

In basketball it goes in the basket,
In rugby the ball goes between the poles
That's how you score the goals,
Tennis is not the same,
It's a completely different game,
You hit the ball to and fro,
If it rains it'll be cancelled though.

You strike the ball into the net
That's how you do it in football,
1-0, 2-0, 3-0, 4-0 and more.

Joseph Quinn-Toye (10)
St Helen's Primary School, Condorrat

Colours

Blue is the colour of royal, sapphire and navy
Brown is the colour of newly made gravy
Yellow is the colour of the hot, lovely sun
While gold is the colour of cakes just done!

Green is the colour of just-cut grass
White is the colour of yummy potato mash
Black is the colour of sophisticated and smart
And lots of different colours are used in art.

Ruby, sapphire, onyx and topaz
Are all precious stones
Which kings and queens get
Studded on their thrones.

Colours, colours as bright
As the stars above
But no one knows which one
Is the colour of love.

Colours make you happy
Like the smell of just cooked bread
And they make you as warm
As snuggling up in your bed.

Blue has royal, sapphire and navy
As I already said
Red has pink, burgundy
And deep, deep red.

Yellow has dandelion,
Pastel and gold.
Green has pastel, metallic
And the colour of mould!

Brown has just that one shade
And black just doesn't easily fade.
Colours are always really, really great
And always want to make people love not hate.

Lisa Agyako (10)
St Helen's Primary School, Condorrat

World War II

I like the war, it's alright,
But something I like more, is to write,
I bought a diary so red and fair,
So I can write the war memories in there.
My dad is in the World War II
So I don't know what to do.

Writing in my diary with tears dripping down,
I don't feel happy, so I just frown,
I hear a bomb *bang,*
As the silence sang,
I jump to the window, to see what's happened,
The smoke builds up like a cold, foggy day,
It doesn't feel the same when Dad's away.

All the violence in one day,
I hope and hope that Dad's okay.
Grandad died in World War I
So Dad is going in the war to copy because he's his son.

A bang smashes against the door
It's Dad!
I knew he wouldn't be hurt.
I shouldn't have been so sad.
I'm relieved and filled with joy,
He's got lots of stories to tell me
And I am happy he's back!

Joanne O'Neill (10)
St Helen's Primary School, Condorrat

My Favourite Food

I like food, it is very yummy
And it fills my hungry tummy
Some of it is healthy, some of it is not
Lots of it is cold and lots of it is hot.

I like sausages, they're not healthy at all
Stewed or fried I'd eat them all
I should eat healthy food
Oh yes I should.

Sandwiches are nice
They have no spice
I also love chicken
Especially the greasy pickin'.

When I am hungry I like to eat curry
But not when I am in a hurry
It spills everywhere
And a white top isn't good to wear.

My favourite curry is as spicy as a bowl of chillies
Last, but not least
It is fishy tuna
So good for a hungry Buddha.

That is all my favourite food
I should eat food
Oh yes I should.

Katie O'Connor (10)
St Helen's Primary School, Condorrat

The Drama Queen

I used to know a drama queen,
Who had hair like an ice cream,
She had it tied back in a bun,
Her yellow hair shimmered in the sun.
Her name was Hannah, Hannah Banana.
She had a pink tutu and shiny pink shoes
That she used to always use.

She was in all the school plays and went to drama every day.
She was the best at drama in her class.
Drama was her favourite subject.
Her mum and dad were very proud
And at the plays they cheered out loud.
She played Cinderella, Sleeping Beauty and Pocahontas too.

When she was sixteen she was in a car crash
And wasn't able to act for two years, her family was in tears.
When she was better she decided to quit.
The drama queen moved away the next day.
Her awesome acts were no more
Because now she works in a shopping store.

Hannah Moore (10)
St Helen's Primary School, Condorrat

A Football Craze

It's the day of the big football final,
And we are playing against the awesome Rhynos,
They are as fierce as a tiger ready to pounce on a zebra.

I've woken up, got changed into my strip,
I peep through the window and *hooray!*
It's scorching hot outside.

I have been down the stairs, had my breakfast,
And I've got my flashy football boots on,
For my breakfast I had a tattie scone.

We are off to the game and I have no pains,
The game's started and no one's departed,
The whistle blows for half-time, still nil-nil
I feel guilty because I am the super striker
And I haven't scored a goal!

Second half begins and *goal!*
We're one-nil up and it was Cammy who scored the goal
Ninety minutes gone, another *goal!*
It's me who scores the goal this time!

Mark Kennedy (10)
St Helen's Primary School, Condorrat

Frosty Feeling

Winter is here,
Give a festive cheer!
Put a smile on,
Christmas is near.

The leaves that are thick,
Lie silently on the thick layer of snow on the ground,
At night can you hear the werewolves hound?

The robins that are red,
Burst into song when you are in bed.
They survive the frost, cold and snow,
Whilst we are sitting in front of the fire,
Our heart's desire.

The warm woolly hat,
Is not on the rack,
It's down on our heads instead
To keep us warm from the icy blast,
Or the avalanche or the mast.

When I step outside,
I feel as cold as the ice surrounding my path,
Meanwhile my sister feels like a hot bath.

I come back home,
Cosy and snug,
I jump into bed
And feel like a bug in a rug.

Farran Smith (10)
St Helen's Primary School, Condorrat

The Schooldays

When I was at school,
It was like a whirlpool,
Most people played, but some of them stayed.

When we were doing maths,
We got as hot and sweaty as a steamy bubble bath.
Our JRSO,
Goes out in the snow,
To keep us safe from the speeders,
Because they're not our leaders.

When I hear the bell,
I run and tell,
The friends of mine,
That it is time,
To take a big stride,
And get inside.

When it's time for lunch,
I go and munch.
I sit on the chair beside my friends
And trade my KitKat
For their chocolate blend.

I go to school to get educated,
And my mum told me that, that was clearly stated.
I go to school five days a week,
I put on my school shoes,
They're small and sleek.

Caitlin Rennie (10)
St Helen's Primary School, Condorrat

Little Dancer

Cassie Ballet loves to dance,
She goes out to sing and prance.
She lives on a farm next to empty fields
And there she dances with her dog Eel.

She wears a leotard as silky as her hair
And a tutu as wide as a bear!
Her hair in a bun, diamonds in her ears,
You'll know if she's far or near.

Her parents spoil their little girl,
With dance shoes and many pearls.
On her walls, in her room, she has many posters
And she loves being on a poster.

But one day when her dad sold his farm,
She lost her fields to dance in.
She moved to a bigger house,
But a smaller garden.

She still loves to dance,
But she has found more interesting things.

Claire Haughey (10)
St Helen's Primary School, Condorrat

My Birthday

My birthday was very good,
It put me in a good mood,
Everybody turned up,
Even though we had lots of chocolates,
Nobody threw up.

My party was as wonderful as half a dozen Smarties.
The gifts were all very nice.
Even though it was a high price,
But I said thank you about a hundred times.

My age was nine,
But I wish I was ten
Because my big sister's friend,
Always calls me her hen.

As I get older she'll stop it,
Or at least, I hope
Because I don't think I can cope.
But anyway, at least I had a good party,
As tasty as a Smartie.

Sophie Gilbride (9)
St Helen's Primary School, Condorrat

Animals In The Zoo

In the mighty jungle the tiger sleeps
And its dinner weeps.
It weeps because it is going to go to
Get beaten and also eaten.

The elephant makes the ground rumble,
While the lion is the king of the jungle,
The lion is loud,
The elephant is eager to get out of the zoo,
The giraffe is eager too.

The penguins waddle past the noisy seals,
The zebra is a lovely creature,
With a beautiful, stripy feature.

Rabbits are in their green field,
Flopping about and in their hut,
People always tut to say,
That cute little rabbit has run away.

This is the end of my poem
And it is sad to say,
That I have to go away from the zoo,
And the animals think so too.

Chloe Shields (10)
St Helen's Primary School, Condorrat

Christmas Is Great

You walk down the stairs and open the door,
You get a big surprise!
You see lots of presents everywhere and the table
Has plates of beef and mince pies!

You hear the bell go ding-dong,
Rush to the door.
The people come in and give you a present,
You can't get enough, you just want more.

At dinner all the crackers go *bang!*
You tell the joke and everyone goes, 'ha, ha, ha.'
Christmas is great, Christmas is fun.

When dinner is finished you go and get
A cup of tea and a hot mince pie.
When the kettle is boiling you take the time
To pour your mum a glass of wine.

When you go to bed,
Comes to my eye is a tear,
Christmas is ended,
But it will be here next year!

Emma McColl (10)
St Helen's Primary School, Condorrat

Badminton

The racket in my hand, shuttlecock in the air.
Hit the net it must not dare.
You have to hit as hard as a rock hitting the sea,
There's no time to sit and have tea.

If someone hits it hard back to you,
You have to be as fast as a flash of lightning
To get to the back of the court.
But if it goes over the line hitting it, you must abort.

If you win, you feel proud
But if you lose you feel despair.
Also, if you win a match and cheer out loud!
But also If you lose it becomes like you don't care.

I go to badminton,
You should too.
But if you don't like it you can say boo!
But I'd go if I were you.

Caitlin Divers (10)
St Helen's Primary School, Condorrat

It's Christmas

It's Christmas, it's Christmas, it's Christmas hooray.
I'm going to invite my friends to stay.
We'll play games, have fun, stay up late too
And now I'll put on my home-made stew.

I'll wrap up the presents before they come,
I've got sweets and chocolate, yum, yum, yum.
There's loads to see on Christmas Day,
It's the best time of the year, hip hip hooray!

It's going to be snowing, I heard it on the news,
But I still can't think what to choose.
It's either 'Charlie and the Chocolate Factory' DVD
Or 'George of the Jungle in the Sea'.

The snow is glittering on the wet ground,
I see a robin singing his sweetest sound!
I feel happy and excited too,
I know it's going to be the best Christmas, don't you?

Juliette Carson
St Helen's Primary School, Condorrat

The Wind Is Like A . . .

The wind is like a snake
It slithers and swoops
It whispers round the window
And *crash!* It pulls off the roof.

The wind is like a Mexican bull
It rams cars in the air
And pushes down my door
It flips the tiles off the roof too.

The wind is like a wolf
It roars, growls and wrecks the place
It crashes down and puts through a wall
But manages not to wake the flowers.

But when it's put together
The slithering snake, the Mexican bull and the roaring wolf
It creates a huge hurricane
Crash! Thunder! Roar! Slither!

But the next morning it's finished making a natural disaster
It whispers down the road
Looking for another place to blow
And to crash, to thunder, to roar, to slither.

Charlie McGleenan (10)
St Jarlath's Primary School, Blackwatertown

The Storm

One dark night I heard a noise,
A loud noise.
It sounded like a storm coming.
I called for help.
The TV news said the storm
Was ten minutes from Armagh.

The next day I ran to Armagh,
Nothing had changed!

Bradley Dynes (10)
St Jarlath's Primary School, Blackwatertown

The Wind

The wind is a furious dragon,
Instead of fire, he blows air.
You can always feel his presence.
You can always see his glare.

He will turn the calm seas.
He will rip all the roofs.
The horses will neigh
And gallop away.

He will cut the grass,
With his sharp blades.
He will dig up the soil,
With his shovels and spades.

When all is quiet
And night turns to day,
The wind whispers,
As it blows away.

Shannen Hughes (11)
St Jarlath's Primary School, Blackwatertown

Roaring Wind

Houses with weak foundations
I will lift with all my might
I'm unstoppable, I'll destroy all.

Light motorbikes
I will tear apart, engines I'll destroy
I'm unstoppable, I'll destroy all.

Coastlands below water level
I will flood with all my might
I'm unstoppable, I'll destroy.

Anthony Mackle (11)
St Jarlath's Primary School, Blackwatertown

The Power Of The Wind . . .

Houses I will destroy
I, the wind, so powerful
I will destroy everything.

Cars I will tear apart
I, the wind, so powerful
I will destroy everything.

Trees I will strike
I, the wind, I, so powerful
I will destroy everything.

Boats I will sink
I, the wind, I, so powerful
I will destroy everything.

Schools I will destroy for the children
I, the wind, I, so powerful.
I will destroy everything.

Tony Doherty (11)
St Jarlath's Primary School, Blackwatertown

The Whistling Wind

He can move around the world,
He can destroy everything
He is powerful.

He can lock up houses.
He can make angry sounds.
He can roar and whistle.

The wind is unstoppable.
He can whisper down the road.
He can drive storm clouds
And shake all towers.

Nayana Mary Saju (12)
St Jarlath's Primary School, Blackwatertown

The Wind Is Like A Dragon

The wind is like a dragon,
It's powerful and loud,
It whistles right past you
And makes the biggest sound.

The wind is unstoppable,
It mostly comes out at night,
If you open your front door,
It will give you the biggest bite.

The wind is sometimes tired
And sometimes like a breeze,
But when it gets louder,
It will swish you off your feet.

The wind is sometimes angry
And fights against the heat,
But when it comes to a hot summer's day,
I think it has a little sleep.

Aoife McKenna (10)
St Jarlath's Primary School, Blackwatertown

The Powerful Wind

The wind is like a lion
That roars through the chimney.

It can strip off the leaves
Of that old oak tree.

Then it comes roaring through the town
And wrecking all the things without a sound.

Then the next morning the wind is still near
And it's still whistling over here.

Then it scatters to the next town
And destroys all the things never to be found.

Louise Donnelly (10)
St Jarlath's Primary School, Blackwatertown

Crashing Wind

The wind is a lion
Always roaring in the sky
Every day it passes
It wrecks as it goes by.

The wind is like a machine
Tearing everything it sees
Scattering all the little birds
From their homes in the trees.

The wind is so powerful
As powerful as could be
And if you go to face it
It will knock you off your feet.

The wind is unstoppable
Destroying all in its way
So you'd better be careful
You could be in danger some day.

Emma Rafferty (10)
St Jarlath's Primary School, Blackwatertown

The Roaring Wind

The wind is like a jaguar,
That strips the leaves off trees,
It can wreck cars,
Or even houses it will tear apart.

Then it starts crashing down alleyways,
Scattering bins from side to side.
Whistling through streets and knocking things down,
Knocking down barriers in the town.

Then it slows down and doesn't make a sound,
It will be back, I know that for sure.

Ryan Hughes (10)
St Jarlath's Primary School, Blackwatertown

The Power Of Wind

The wind is a roaring beast,
Blowing from the west to the east,
He can be nice or gentle or kind,
Or even have more fierce things in mind.

He can rant and he can rave,
To go out in him you must be brave,
Trampolines, swings or even slides,
May come across his evil side.

Nothing can stand in his way,
He can blow night or day,
Please be careful when he is there,
Because he can wreck more than hair.

If you leave him then he'll leave you,
If you provoke him it could be the last thing you do,
So keep away when he's around,
Or else there might be more than sound.

Laura Finn (11)
St Jarlath's Primary School, Blackwatertown

Wind

The wind is like a stallion.
Mad, crazy and out of control.

The wind is like a digger.
It can lift things off the ground.

The wind is like a bulldozer.
It can push things out of its way.

Liam McKenna (10)
St Jarlath's Primary School, Blackwatertown

The Mighty Wind

The wind is an angry pit bull
That destroys little birds' nests
And scatters litter over the street
With his powerful mouth.

He's whistling under all your doors
That sounds like ghosts
And swishing up the stairs
To scatter things everywhere.

Hitting the windows in anger
Wrecking your plants and flowers
Lifting up your trampoline like a frisbee
And crashing it through the trees.

Next morning he's still there
But he has died down
Then he moves to another place
To blow with all his might.

Chloe Starkey (11)
St Jarlath's Primary School, Blackwatertown

The Wind Is An Animal

The wind is a horse
It gallops through the sky
You can see it, you can hear it
As it goes right by.

The wind is an elephant
It is big and it is loud,
If it steps, it will squash
It goes as high as the clouds.

The wind is a crocodile
It goes snap, snap, snap
It crawls all around you
And goes in through the cat flap.

The wind is so powerful
The wind can destroy,
Children do not play with it
It is not a toy.

Niamh McElroy (11)
St Jarlath's Primary School, Blackwatertown

I, The Wind

I, the wind, will make your garden untidy,
Move your trees and pots,
I, the wind, will lift your trampoline
And put your ropes in knots.

I, the wind, can scatter leaves,
Destroy your buildings and walls,
I, the wind, can also cause nasty falls.

I, the wind, will make you flee
And make you have nowhere to go,
I, the wind, will rattle your keys
And destroy everything you know.

So watch out for my power
For I may come to you,
Even when you least expect it
I might blow you away too.

Michelle Graham (11)
St Jarlath's Primary School, Blackwatertown

I'm Just Going To School

'I'm just going to school.'
'Why?'
'Because I've got to learn.'
'Why?'
'Because I'm not poorly.'
'Why?'
'Because I'm healthy.'
'Why?'
'Because I eat lots of fruit.'
'Why?'
'Stop saying why please.'
'Why?'
'Because you're giving me a headache!'

Hero Gough (7)
St Mark's Elm Tree CE VA Primary School, Fairfield

I'm Just Going To Bed

'I'm just going to bed.'
'Why?'
'Because I'm tired.'
'Why?'
'Because I've been working all day.'
'Why?'
'Because I stayed up late last night.'
'Why?'
'Because I had lots of work to do.'
'Why?'
'Because I spent more time with you at the weekend.'
'Why?'
'Would you stop saying why.'
'Why?'
'Because you are annoying me.'
'OK I'll say what!'

Anna Levin (8)
St Mark's Elm Tree CE VA Primary School, Fairfield

I'm Going To The Park

'I'm going to the park.'
'Why?'
'To go quad biking.'
'Why?'
'Because it is fun.'
'Why?'
'Because it is fast.'
'Why?'
'Because it has a big engine.'

William Noble (7)
St Mark's Elm Tree CE VA Primary School, Fairfield

I'm Just Going To Bed

'I'm just going to bed.'
'Why?'
'Because I am sleepy.'
'Why?'
'I have been doing my homework.'
'Why?'
'Because it's for school.'
'Why?'
'It helps me learn.'

Chloe Hooker (7)
St Mark's Elm Tree CE VA Primary School, Fairfield

I'm Thin But I Eat

I'm thin but I eat,
I eat lots of meat,
But now I'm too fat
To fit in my seat!

Kerys Dodsworth (7)
St Mark's Elm Tree CE VA Primary School, Fairfield

I'm Just Going In The Garden

'I'm just going in the garden.'
'Why?'
'Because the flowers are thirsty.'
'Why?'
'Because it hasn't rained in ages.'
'Why?'
'Because it's hot outside.'
'Why?'
'Because it is summer.'

Danielle Russell & Courtney Edgar (7)
St Mark's Elm Tree CE VA Primary School, Fairfield

I Was Late Because . . .

I was late home because . . .
I was talking to my friends.
I was late home because . . .
I got stuck in traffic.
I was late home because . . .
I had to finish my work.
I was late home because . . .
I walked a different way home.

Ashleigh Helen Wilkinson (7)
St Mark's Elm Tree CE VA Primary School, Fairfield

The Sun

The shining ball of fire in the sky
Is like a pie in the sky.
The shining ball of fire is still alive.
A sparkler is like a big yellow sun.

Daniel Harbron (7)
St Mark's Elm Tree CE VA Primary School, Fairfield

The Sun

The shining ball of fire in the sky,
The sun is like a big pie.
If you look at it,
It will damage your eye,
It will make you cry.

James Southwick-Hawkes (8)
St Mark's Elm Tree CE VA Primary School, Fairfield

The Sun

The sun is a yellow ball of fire.
It is very, very bright.
If you look at the sun
You can damage your eyes.
Some people get burnt.

Nicole Banthorpe (7)
St Mark's Elm Tree CE VA Primary School, Fairfield

You Asked Me Why I Wanted To Be Rich

You asked me why I wanted to be rich
Because I wanted lots of jewellery.
You asked me why I wanted lots of jewellery
Because I will look nice.
You asked me why I wanted to look nice
Because everyone will like me.
I would like that.

Joe Garratt (7)
St Mark's Elm Tree CE VA Primary School, Fairfield

The Sun

The shining ball of fire in the sky,
The sun is like a big yellow pie.
The sun is as round as the pupil in your eye.
It can make you cry.
So bye.

Jonathon Blackwell (8)
St Mark's Elm Tree CE VA Primary School, Fairfield

Light Poem

F lickering in the dark
L ight so bright
A lone in the window
M agnificent bright light
E xcellent shining light.

Alex Clothier & Danielle Stewart (7)
St Martin's Garden Primary School, Odd Down

Ten Things Found In A Fairy's Pocket

A child's tooth,
A sprinkle of magic fairy dust,
A tiny shoe,
A flower petal hat,
A magic wand,
A spare pair of wings,
A happy spell,
A bumblebee to fly with,
A pound to pay for a tooth,
A lucky star.

Keshia Morgan (8)
St Martin's Garden Primary School, Odd Down

Light Poem

F lames wiggle around in the dark
L ike sparkles of light
A t night the shadows look like black ghosts
M um lights the candle to make everyone feel calm
E veryone goes to sleep. Goodnight!

Jordan Norton (7)
St Martin's Garden Primary School, Odd Down

Ten Things Found In A Witch's Pocket

A bottle of poison,
A big black cat,
A handy wand,
A huge broomstick,
A book of spells,
Slugs for a snack,
Snails for a poison,
A rat's tail,
A cauldron,
A bird beak pen.

Laura Nettle (8)
St Martin's Garden Primary School, Odd Down

My Leaf

My leaf is yellow and spotty
It looks like a ghost
It smells like figs and apricots
It reminds me of Christmas.

Leah Redpath Smith (10)
St Martin's Garden Primary School, Odd Down

Ten Things Found In A Policeman's Pocket

A pair of handcuffs,
A gun to shoot,
A pot of ink for fingerprints,
A note pad and pen,
A magnifying glass,
A pair of glasses,
A radio for help,
A whistle to blow,
A sandwich to eat,
A big bunch of keys.

Simeon Wakely (9)
St Martin's Garden Primary School, Odd Down

Light Poem

L ight flickers
I n the dark
G rowing bigger and brighter
H ot and shimmering
T winkling in the dark.

Ellie Marchant & Courtney Jones (7)
St Martin's Garden Primary School, Odd Down

The Flame

The flame flickers
In the night like a
Colourful shadow.
The flame is like a
Fiery raindrop.

F lames flicker
L ight dazzles
A lone in the night
M elting starts to happen
E veryone is happy.

Isabel Vinall & Alisa White
St Martin's Garden Primary School, Odd Down

Winter

Winter is cold and frosty,
Winter is snowballs and snowmen,
Winter is Christmas time,
Winter is a white blanket on the ground,
Winter is the time for holly and berries,
Winter is the best time ever!

Rebecca Erm (8)
St Martin's Garden Primary School, Odd Down

Ten Things Found In A Devil's Pocket

A fork,
A list of horrible people,
A bottle of dust,
A ball of fire,
A rotten skull,
A clipper to clip long nails,
An eyeball,
A pot of blood,
A rotten tooth,
A wicked spell.

Daniel Flatters (8)
St Martin's Garden Primary School, Odd Down

Ten Things Found In A Teacher's Pocket

A rubber to rub out mistakes,
House points for when we're good,
A pencil to write with,
Pens to mark the register,
A whistle for PE,
A stopwatch for PE,
A spelling test - oh no!
A cup for tea for break,
A small computer,
A bright idea for our homework!

Carley Morgan (8)
St Martin's Garden Primary School, Odd Down

Sea Fever

I must go down to the sea today
to hear the gulls cry as loud and thrilling as a wolf.
To listen to the waves crash into the rocks
like a steam train thundering by at full speed.

I must go down to the sea today
to feel the sand beneath my toes like thick mud.
To feel the rod in my hands
and the big fish wriggling in my arms.

I must go down to the sea today
to see the gold glowing sand.
To see the bluey green of the clear water.

I must go down to the sea today
to do what I do best . . .
                              Relax!

Jerram Hall (11)
St Mary's Catholic Primary School, Buckfast

Six Different Ways Of Looking At Sheep

Above me I see white sheep jumping around with joy.
Around me the sheep talk happily through the grass.
Behind me I see the sheep bleating in the sun as it rises.
Beside me is a lamb eating my shorts.
Under me the sheep play nicely around my legs as they get dirty.
Over the hill I look back as I leave the field of sheep for home.

Jesse Major (9)
St Mary's Catholic Primary School, Buckfast

Four Ways Of Looking At The Sky

In the water I see a fire in the sky, I think it's trying to
tell me something.
Over there I see my sheep dancing in the orange light of the fire
in the sky.
Above the hills I see a tree with leaves dancing in the light of the fire
in the sky.
In my robe I see a part of a message, I think this is what the fire
was trying to tell me!

Ryan Butler (11)
St Mary's Catholic Primary School, Buckfast

Five Ways To Look At Ashburton

Before me I see a peaceful little town filled with fresh air
and smooth walls, with gold and yellow on the walls.
Over me I see a lovely blue sky, high as high.
Under my feet I feel the hard, hilly roads.
Beside me I see loads of tall houses reaching, up, up and up.
Around me I see friendly, happy people.

Dylan Crisp (9)
St Mary's Catholic Primary School, Buckfast

My Brother's Bedroom!

My brother's bedroom, it's never clean, it's such a scene.
I hate my brother's bedroom, he has so many things.
He takes his toys apart but that's just the start.
Then he loses everything and gets in a mood.
He does not care about the mess, it's never going to change.
To be honest, I'm quite used to Mum getting in a rage
                                    because of the mess he's made.

Chloé Fox (9)
St Mary's Catholic Primary School, Buckfast

The Bear

The bear is as fierce as a volcano and runs as fast as a cheetah.
He tells jokes that make you laugh like a hyena,
he has teeth as sharp as knives and claws as sharp as swords
and his stomping feet make earthquakes all over the world!

Charles John William Roper (9)
St Mary's Catholic Primary School, Buckfast

Under My Bed

Under my bed there's a whole load of things,
From an old pink cap to a butterfly's wings,
A packet of crisps and a mouldy old shoe,
A new science set and a hamster's poo,
My old fluffy bear and some other stuff,
A hole in my bed spills out dusty, grey fluff,
And when I'm told to clear it out,
I'll stuff it in the cupboard, no doubt.

Jesse Thompson (10)
St Mary's Catholic Primary School, Buckfast

The Good Shepherd

Above the hills, the flames of God from the setting sun.
Under my feet the river of love reflects the Lamb of God.
The Good Shepherd looks after His sheep under the flames of God.
The Good Shepherd looks after His sheep, never letting them go.
Above the sheep is the Staff of Life; if a sheep is stuck, the
                                        Staff hooks it out.

Howard Ellacott (9)
St Mary's Catholic Primary School, Buckfast

Ways Of Looking In My Wardrobe

Go! Go! Look inside,
you might get a shocking surprise,
Is it my skeleton, is it my cat,
Or is it Beavas, my pet rat?

That's just three things you might find,
inside that dark cupboard of mine,
there are mouldy cakes
and grass snakes,
that might make you shake.

'Amy, Amy, don't go in there,
I don't want to explain to Mum,
why you got a scare.'

George Lowrey (10)
St Mary's Catholic Primary School, Buckfast

Three Ways To Look At Humans

Beside me I see myself with different feelings, but with no mirror.
Same blue eyes, same pink ears, same pale complexion and
soft blonde hair.

Across the field I see the man that sheared me and took my warmth.
Killed my mate Bertie and sold him still attached to the bone.

Below me I see them, just about, so small, so strong.
They tell me to go away if ever I drop the clear substance that
anchors me to the ground.
They predict me so often, and fly through me even more, with the
mechanical flying machines.

Emily Loxton & Florrie Connell (10)
St Mary's Catholic Primary School, Buckfast

A Good Headmistress

Below the sky is a school,
In it is a headmistress,
She is nice and kind,
She is good at working with children.
Her hugs are big and warm,
You can be a good friend to her,
And she will be a good friend to you,
So don't be afraid, she will see you as a good
worker!

Bethani-Rose Butler (10)
St Mary's Catholic Primary School, Buckfast

Christmas Eve

The night before Christmas
Was a very dark night,
All I could see was the moon's lovely light.

The night before Christmas
And all I could see,
Were the shining lights on the Christmas tree.

The night before Christmas
And all I could feel,
Was the fluffy white snow under my heel.

The night before Christmas
I heard bells ring
And the songs of the choir filled the church as they sung.

The night before Christmas
Santa was here,
I could hear the hooves of Rudolph the reindeer.

Joanna Townley (9)
St Mary's CE Primary School, Prestwich

Trench Warfare

The screaming of the wing sandwich biplane issues ear-breakingly
Over the soldiers' helmets,
The artillery blasts the trench barriers endlessly,
The thumping of the soldiers' feet throbs all over no-man's-land,
The soldiers creep carefully across the many minefields,
Explosions range across the dark skies,
Blimps fly across the sky, dropping bombs onto the
Barren wasteland,
Machine guns, the size of a caber, lie broken and unused
Over the muddy plains.

Trench warfare.

Max McGinn (9)
St Mary's CE Primary School, Prestwich

Skeleton

Bony skeleton.
White, bony skeleton.
Scary, white, bony skeleton
Rattling through the night.
Skeleton.

Siobhan Turnbull (7)
St Mary's Primary School, Bonnyrigg

Skeleton

Rattling skeleton.
White, rattling skeleton.
Dancing, white, rattling skeleton
Hanging from a beam.
Skeleton.

Liam Lothian (8)
St Mary's Primary School, Bonnyrigg

Skeleton

Bony skeleton,
Rattling, bony skeleton,
Scary, rattling, bony skeleton,
Doing a dance all night.
Skeleton.

Beatrice Begg (8)
St Mary's Primary School, Bonnyrigg

Skeleton

Bony skeleton
White, bony skeleton
Naked, white, bony skeleton
Wobbling in a cave.
Skeleton.

Glenn Wood (8)
St Mary's Primary School, Bonnyrigg

Skeleton

Black-hearted skeleton
Brainless, black-hearted skeleton
Scary, brainless, black-hearted skeleton
Haunting in a scary mansion.
Skeleton.

Mattia Emiliana Ocone (7)
St Mary's Primary School, Bonnyrigg

Skeleton

Naked skeleton
Eyeless, naked skeleton.
Scary, eyeless, naked skeleton
Scaring people away.

Aaron Milne (8)
St Mary's Primary School, Bonnyrigg

Skeleton

Naked skeleton.
Skinless, naked skeleton.
Bony, skinless, naked skeleton.
Scaring a little boy.
Skeleton.

Sean Cocker (7)
St Mary's Primary School, Bonnyrigg

Skeleton

Bony skeleton
White, bony skeleton.
Naked, white, bony skeleton
Playing in his cave.
Skeleton.

Nicole Rutherford (8)
St Mary's Primary School, Bonnyrigg

Skeleton

Naked skeleton
Bony, naked skeleton.
Hopeless, bony, naked skeleton
Flopping about in the cave.
Skeleton.

Hailey McCulloch (7)
St Mary's Primary School, Bonnyrigg

Skeleton

Bony skeleton.
Rattling, bony skeleton.
Black-hearted, rattling, bony skeleton
Scaring people through the night.
Skeleton.

Matthew Graham (8)
St Mary's Primary School, Bonnyrigg

Skeleton

Brainless skeleton.
Bony, brainless skeleton.
White, bony, brainless skeleton
Lying dead in a haunted house.
Skeleton.

T J Connell (8)
St Mary's Primary School, Bonnyrigg

Skeleton

Hopeless skeleton.
Naked, hopeless skeleton.
Rattling, naked, hopeless skeleton
Rattling through the haunted castle.
Skeleton.

Darren McBay (8)
St Mary's Primary School, Bonnyrigg

The New Girl

I am bubbly and snuggly
Yet I'm lost and left out
I am tired and I'm alone
I'm frightened, I'm the new girl

I want to be happy
But I am so sad
I am sometimes joyful
When you are about
I am all alone

In the playground
They say to me, 'Oh look!
There's the new girl'
And they point at me

Then one day someone came
They said, 'Hey, wanna play?'

Alice Urwin (10)
SS Wulstan's & Edmund's Catholic Primary School & Nursery, Fleetwood

Space

S   is for stars shining,
like a diamond ring in the blackness of the night sky,

P   is for Pluto,
the last planet,
that feels as cold as an ice lolly that has just come out of the freezer,

A   is for asteroids,
speeding through the galaxy,
like racing cars

C   is for comets,
zooming so fast,
they leave a magical trail behind them.

E   is for the Earth,
that looks like it has been painted by a famous painter.

Megan Bennett-Tipping (10)
SS Wulstan's & Edmund's Catholic Primary School & Nursery, Fleetwood

Space Poem

Space
with black, leathery wings
engulfing all.

So empty
alone
dark
deep

yet so full.

Light
lively
powerful.

With the comets

travelling
ever so fast
on their padded, soft, cat feet.

And the meteors
drifting
huge
wide
immense.

The stars
crackling
so massive
everything is in awe.

The planets
as different as humans
small
wide
mighty
cold
melting.

I think space is, above all, wondrous.

Connor McGladdery (10)
SS Wulstan's & Edmund's Catholic Primary School & Nursery, Fleetwood

Trees

Trees swaying in the
Wind on a beautiful autumn day
Trees cold as ice on a chilly winter's day
Trees are all around us all year round
Trees, peaceful as the birds on a sunny spring day
Trees stand tall and straight on a hot summer's day
Trees, we need them to live
Trees are great
Trees.

T
R
E
E
S
T
R
E
E
S

Trees are just that . . . *trees!*

Conor Kaye (10)
SS Wulstan's & Edmund's Catholic Primary School & Nursery, Fleetwood

Tsunami

Raging up onto the surface like an angry bull.
Racing to a destination like a cheetah.
Destroying everything in its way like a lion killing its prey.
Forcing everyone to evacuate like a herd of elephants.
Deafening everyone in its way like a volcano about to erupt.
Storming around the city like a meteor that has just fallen.
Calming down like a dog panting.

Jack Conneely (10)
SS Wulstan's & Edmund's Catholic Primary School & Nursery, Fleetwood

Storming Down The Stairs

Storming down the stairs
Like a raging bull
Storming down the stairs
Swelling eyes are full

Thundering down the stairs
Like a roaring gale
Thundering down the stairs
Like bouncing hail

Storming down the stairs
A moody child
Storming down the stairs
Mad, angry, irate and wild

Thundering down the stairs
My anger has not gone
At the bottom of the stairs
My sister! What has she done?

Faye Simpson (10)
SS Wulstan's & Edmund's Catholic Primary School & Nursery, Fleetwood

My Family

My family is loud as a lion
When they talk.
My family may be greedy
When they need to be.
My family are all as bouncy as springs.
My family is crazy like the 'Crazy Frog'.
My family are all loonies like me.
My family loves each other.

Thomas Greenall (9)
SS Wulstan's & Edmund's Catholic Primary School & Nursery, Fleetwood

My Best Friend Chloe

Her eyes are like rare blue diamonds.
Her hair is like a curtain of red silk,
glittering in the light.
She's a fluffy pillow on which I
lay my head.
She's a graceful dolphin
swimming in the sunset.
She's a cheeky monkey swinging
in a tree.
She is a tall lighthouse,
guiding me when I'm lost.
An energy drink,
a pogo stick,
and my best friend.

Lucinda Denney (10)
SS Wulstan's & Edmund's Catholic Primary School & Nursery, Fleetwood

My Friend Alice

I have a friend named Alice,
When we're older we'll share a palace.
We play together night and day,
No matter what other people say!

As friends are for sticking together,
Friends forever, enemies never,
Friends are supposed to make each other kinder,
Together we help her mum - a childminder.

Friends always help each other the most,
But we stick together no matter what the cost.
When we fall out it really hurts,
All my tears begin to burst!

Chloe Atkinson (10)
SS Wulstan's & Edmund's Catholic Primary School & Nursery, Fleetwood

Babies

Babies' blankets are soft little teddies.
Their smiles are cute, little, pink pencils
drawn onto peach paper.
Their bodies are little costumes
hiding their insides.
Their sounds are radios making
giggles when they can.
Their eyes are two little coloured sponges
that look everywhere,
up, down, left and right.
Their smile is sweeter than strawberry ice cream.
This is what a baby means to me,
is this what a baby means to you?

Jenny Mottershead (9)
SS Wulstan's & Edmund's Catholic Primary School & Nursery, Fleetwood

My Best Friend

My best friend is so crazy.
Not dumb and not that lazy.

My best friend is very funny.
She has a fluffy white bunny.

My best friend can be so mad.
She cheers me up when I'm sad.

My best friend is so jumpy.
Not soft and not lumpy.

My best friend is so cool.
She even has her own pool.

But, best of all, she's called *Amy.*

Emily Brand (9)
SS Wulstan's & Edmund's Catholic Primary School & Nursery, Fleetwood

The Dragon

There is one dragon,
His name is Bracken,
A dragon is a glorious creature,
He soars through the air,
He beats his powerful wings,
Which are bigger than a bear,
A dragon is a glorious creature,
Perched on a rock, he sleeps all day,
At night he swims through the ice-cold bay,
A dragon is a glorious creature . . .

But then hunters arrived,
He managed to miss their fiery bullets of death
And survived,
The hunters all left,
His life had been kept.

There is only one dragon left,
And his name is Bracken.

Chloe McLaughlin (10)
SS Wulstan's & Edmund's Catholic Primary School & Nursery, Fleetwood

My Best Friend

I have a friend called Sera,
But sometimes I cannot bear her,
And sometimes we do everything together,
No matter what the weather.

When she sleeps at my house,
She is so not as quiet as a mouse,
But when I sleep at her house,
She sometimes does impressions of a scout.
That is all about me and my friend.
So please tell me who is your friend?

Olivia Darbyshire (10)
SS Wulstan's & Edmund's Catholic Primary School & Nursery, Fleetwood

Grass

Grass, swift as wind blowing gently
Grass, as soft as the fluff of the finest cushions
Grass, as sweet as the whistling of the greatest flute
Grass, as strong as a bull charging in a theatre ring
Grass, a beautiful thing and should not be underestimated.

James Delaney (9)
SS Wulstan's & Edmund's Catholic Primary School & Nursery, Fleetwood

Sleep Little Baby

The baby's skin is a thin marshmallow,
His hair is a bunch of fluffy feathers,
The baby's smile is an upside down rainbow,
His eyes are blue berries,
The baby's towel is a cloud wrapped around him,
His hands are as delicate as diamonds,
The baby's feet are as soft as a pillow,
His toes are as small as peas.

Jamie Greenall (10)
SS Wulstan's & Edmund's Catholic Primary School & Nursery, Fleetwood

Anger

Anger is red like a fierce, exploding volcano,
It sounds like a drum, pounding in my head,
It tastes like a sour orange squirting through the air,
It looks like a fire blazing through a block of flats,
It feels like a hard rock,
It smells like stale bread.

Faye Eardley
SS Wulstan's & Edmund's Catholic Primary School & Nursery, Fleetwood

Horse

Sparks off his feet
like lightning from the clouds.
Wind blows,
making manes and tails flow like sails.
Soft grass under jabbing hooves,
that sounds like a panther with prey.
He comes close to the great whale depth,
pouncing,
flying like an eagle,
stretching,
touching
and landing.

Libby Tegan Ramsbottom (11)
SS Wulstan's & Edmund's Catholic Primary School & Nursery, Fleetwood

The Wind

The storm rages like an angry lion
The chilling rain pours loudly on my window
The icy hailstones ricochet off the hard, damp ground
And with the blink of an eye, they melt
I see few cars, window wipers flashing madly
The huge tyres drench the kerb
There's not a single person in sight
But I'm sitting on the sofa
With the fire on
Tucking into a hot fudge brownie.

Sophie Shields (10)
SS Wulstan's & Edmund's Catholic Primary School & Nursery, Fleetwood

Cats

Cats are furry but vicious,
But they are very delicious.

Cats have sharp claws,
They also scratch on doors!

Cats get fleas
They never land on their knees.

Cats have tickly whiskers
Paw pads are like blisters.

Cats miaow like thunder
They always blunder!

Amy Taylor (10)
SS Wulstan's & Edmund's Catholic Primary School & Nursery, Fleetwood

Myself And Football

I have scored 17 goals already
And my mate has left, called Eddy,
I really like football,
Although I'm not very small,
Although I shoot from afar,
I like to get it under the crossbar,
I hate the offside rule,
And our team is very cool,
My worst enemy is Cocksall,
And the team I play for is
Foxhall.

Michael Perry (11)
SS Wulstan's & Edmund's Catholic Primary School & Nursery, Fleetwood

Me

I am a strange little boy, as cheeky as can be,
I have lots of friends and I am crazy,
I am funny, imaginative and very loud,
I am small, cool and very proud,
I am as quick as a cheetah, that is true,
I live near the beach like a lot of people do,
I live with my parents, my two sisters too,
But my brother is at uni and he is quite new,
I was born in Blackpool, Vic,
I'm not very thick.

Benedict Tse-Laurence (11)
SS Wulstan's & Edmund's Catholic Primary School & Nursery, Fleetwood

Friends

Friends are kind
Friends are fun
Friends are really just the one.
Friends are cheerful
Friends are jolly
Friends sometimes just act like wallies!
Friends are shooting stars
Friends will still be friends
Even from afar.

Hayley O'Sullivan (9)
SS Wulstan's & Edmund's Catholic Primary School & Nursery, Fleetwood

My Kittens

Greedy as a lion.
Soft as a feather.
Light as air.
Lively as a bear.
Eyes as bright as light.
I just want to hug them all
Through the night.
Each four claws are as sharp as a knife.
Lively as a kite.
But best of all, they sleep tight.

Kirsty Graham (10)
SS Wulstan's & Edmund's Catholic Primary School & Nursery, Fleetwood

Family Poem

We are as loud as a lion when we talk.
We may be greedy when we need to be.
We all are as bouncy as a spring.
We may be crazy when we need to be.
My family is football crazy.
In the night we play fun games.
In the evening we have our food.
My family are like animals at the table.
My family is boring, just like me.

Michael Swann (10)
SS Wulstan's & Edmund's Catholic Primary School & Nursery, Fleetwood

The Racehorse

The horse number 3 behind the line,
Ready to storm, under, over and through,
Tension over all who bet, building up like a wall,
Being built by fifty-thousand men.

Hundreds of hearts, beating rapidly onto their ribs,
Waiting to explode,
Some people lofty, and some timid.

Number 3 dashes out from behind the gate,
Taking the lead.
The crowd cheers,
But as the others catch up the voices fade.

Still in the lead, number 3,
Goes over the first jump.
Hooves hit the ground, like kgs of weight,
Being pulled to a huge height,
And then being dropped to the ground.
Knocking over stacks of hay and straw.
As a raging herd of horses,
Come galloping towards . . . the finishing line!

As the second lap commences,
Several horses fall down, not to mention the riders.
Number 3 is one minute away from fame!
But then he trips and stops completely.
Everything else follows,
Then everywhere falls silent.

Sorrow and doubts fill the air,
On the tracks of fortune for many,
People miserably empty the stadium.
They hope for the best next year.
The horse returns to his stable,
To be cared for and loved
By his owner once more.

Erin Smyth (10
SS Wulstan's & Edmund's Catholic Primary School & Nursery, Fleetwood

My Nan

My nan is a cosy, warm blanket,
A baby lamb, all snug in a rug.
Always there and always aware,
Diamanté eyes, crystal and bright.
Hair the colour of autumn leaves but smooth and short.
A cheesy big grin and straight white teeth,
Always over the moon whenever I'm there.
A cheerful robin on the frosty fence,
Chirping away on a bright blue day.
Floating away on a candyfloss cloud,
An angel's voice singing gracefully and proud.

Olivia Ikeda-Allen (11)
SS Wulstan's & Edmund's Catholic Primary School & Nursery, Fleetwood

Myself

I'm like a big, greedy dog
I make lots of noise in the fog
I'm always a silly clown
I'm as crazy as a bull
I'm irritating in maths
I'm annoying
I'm as loud as a cat
I'm as nasty as a dog in the dark of night
I'm as evil as a vampire driving a car.

Brandon Garrard (10)
SS Wulstan's & Edmund's Catholic Primary School & Nursery, Fleetwood

Blazing Fireworks

Fireworks are stars exploding in the sky,
Fireworks are fireballs that are waiting to be lit,
Sparklers are fizzing as fast as light,
Catherine wheels are spinning tops on your garden fence,
Blazing bonfires are burning as brightly as the sun,
Fireworks are beautiful and no one can disagree.

Michael Lydon (10)
SS Wulstan's & Edmund's Catholic Primary School & Nursery, Fleetwood

I Wanna Be An Olympic Swimmer

I wanna be an Olympic swimmer,
I wanna be a gold medal winner,
I wanna be as fast as a cheetah!
I wanna be a world record beater,
I wanna have my own swimming pool,
I wanna be famous and cool,
I wanna eat a superstar's dinner,
I wanna be an Olympic swimmer.

Lauren Wilkinson (9)
SS Wulstan's & Edmund's Catholic Primary School & Nursery, Fleetwood

I Wanna Be

I wanna be a famous dancer,
I wanna be a great romancer,
I wanna make people full of glee,
I wanna be as beautiful as can be,
I wanna go around in a flashy car,
I wanna be a shimmering star,
I wanna be a celebrity on the TV,
I wanna be as happy as can be.

Louise Ward (10)
SS Wulstan's & Edmund's Catholic Primary School & Nursery, Fleetwood

Anger

Anger is red like a prickly rose,
It sounds like a drum pounding in my head,
It tastes like pouring blood,
It feels like it's a thousand bee stings,
It smells like burning coal,
It looks like a fierce, exploding volcano.

Bethany Walsh (10)
SS Wulstan's & Edmund's Catholic Primary School & Nursery, Fleetwood

Fireworks

Fireworks are shooting rockets,
Fireworks should not be in your pockets,
A firework is a daisy, petals opening in the air,
A firework can be a danger if you don't take care,
A firework is like rainbow flare,
Fireworks are dangerous, so beware,
A firework is a palm tree shot into the air,
But you really, really, must take care.

Bradley Mills (9)
SS Wulstan's & Edmund's Catholic Primary School & Nursery, Fleetwood

Anger

Anger is red like a fierce, exploding volcano,
It's like a drum pounding in my head,
It smells like hot ash, all flaky and burnt,
It feels like needles driving through my heart,
It looks like a tornado crashing through the trees,
It tastes like burning treacle toffee exploding in my mouth.

Ashleigh Blundell (9)
SS Wulstan's & Edmund's Catholic Primary School & Nursery, Fleetwood

Happiness

Happiness is blue like the sky on a summer's day,
It feels like a relaxing bath,
It smells like a fresh quilt,
It looks like a babbling river,
It tastes like a roast dinner.

Jason Stirzaker (10)
SS Wulstan's & Edmund's Catholic Primary School & Nursery, Fleetwood

My Cousin Amy

She's a loud elephant,
She's a bubbly bath,
She's a hyper monkey,
Her smile is a large slice of watermelon,
Her hair is smooth like dark chocolate,
Her eyes are two rare blue diamonds,
She's a jumpy kangaroo,
She's a thin piece of straw,
She's a bird that sings all day,
And she's my lovely cousin.

Andrew Butler (11)
SS Wulstan's & Edmund's Catholic Primary School & Nursery, Fleetwood

What Is A Baby?

The baby's hair is as soft as cuddly cat fur,
The baby's eyes are pale as the sky,
The baby's smell is sweet-smelling perfume,
The baby's blanket is a flying carpet, full of dreams,
When the baby talks it sounds more like singing,
The baby's feet are the size of a goldfish.

Francesca Warder (10)
SS Wulstan's & Edmund's Catholic Primary School & Nursery, Fleetwood

Happiness

Happiness is yellow like the burning sun,
It tastes like smooth, sweet chocolate,
It smells like a butterfly, fluttering about on a summer's day,
It feels like you are floating above the Earth,
It sounds like a sweet bird singing.

Louis Robinson (10)
SS Wulstan's & Edmund's Catholic Primary School & Nursery, Fleetwood

My Teachers

My teacher's name is Mrs Brainy,
She is helped by Mrs Whizz.

Mr Techno's the science teacher,
He fills our test tubes till they fizz.

Mrs Rhyme's the English teacher,
But she's always shouting at Liz.

Then Mr Clever takes us at the end of the day,
For a little quiz.

Connaire Mulgrew (10)
SS Wulstan's & Edmund's Catholic Primary School & Nursery, Fleetwood

I Wanna Be

I wanna be a footballer
I wanna be a great scorer
I wanna play in my team's vest
I wanna be better than all the rest
I wanna make you all look smaller
I wanna be a footballer.

Billy Dollin (9)
SS Wulstan's & Edmund's Catholic Primary School & Nursery, Fleetwood

Tom And Jerry!

In the corner of the room a little rodent rests,
He loves his little house, reckons it's the best!
Every once in a while he comes out to play,
I say every once in a while, I mean every day!
He loves to eat nibbles, crackers and cheese,
Comes up to me and shouts, 'Food now, food please!'
Whenever Mum sees him, she hits him with a broom,
I shout, 'Quick! Quick! Mouse *zooooom . . . !'*

Mum and Dad took action, mouse traps all over the place,
I wanted to play with him but there was no space,
I hid him in the garden shed,
Even made him a tiny mouse-sized bed,
Guess what! They went further and bought a cat,
I looked at it and thought, *wow! You're fat!*
After a while it got bored,
All the food it ate went in its tummy and was stored,
Then when it saw the mouse,
Stomp! Stomp! Stomp!
All over the house,
Finally the cat was backed up to a wall,
The mouse was amazed and felt so very tall,
Then standing on its tail,
The cat let out an almighty wail,
Now when he sees the mouse,
He shakes and says, 'You're the mouse of the house!'

Lauren Scott
SS Wulstan's & Edmund's Catholic Primary School & Nursery, Fleetwood

Happiness

Happiness is yellow like the sunshine,
It smells like a bunch of freshly picked flowers,
It sounds like a sweet melody,
It looks like a rainbow resting over hills,
It tastes like a juicy ice lolly,
It feels like paradise.

Teddi Spearpoint
SS Wulstan's & Edmund's Catholic Primary School & Nursery, Fleetwood

I Wanna Be A Movie Star

I wanna be a movie star
I wanna have a cool flashy car
I wanna be on the big screen
I wanna load of bling bling
I wanna girl who really rules
I wanna see my name go far
I wanna be a movie star.

Oliver Cheetham (9)
SS Wulstan's & Edmund's Catholic Primary School & Nursery, Fleetwood

Sleep Baby Sleep

Baby's hair is as soft as a cuddly teddy bear.
Baby's skin is smoother than a piece of paper.
Baby's eyes are brighter than the sun.
Baby's fingers and toes are balls of cotton wool.
Baby's blanket is a flying carpet.
Baby's smell is sweeter than a strawberry.
Baby's voice is a cuckoo bird.
Baby's legs and arms are as smooth as a baseball bat.

George Benson (9)
SS Wulstan's & Edmund's Catholic Primary School & Nursery, Fleetwood

Anger

Anger is red like a fierce, exploding volcano.
It sounds like a drum pounding in my head.
It feels like knives slashing through your skin.
It smells like black coal burning in a fire.
It looks like toffee boiling in a pan.
It tastes like old and mouldy cottage cheese.

Sammy Drury (11)
SS Wulstan's & Edmund's Catholic Primary School & Nursery, Fleetwood

Anger

Anger is red like a fierce, exploding volcano,
It tastes like burnt toast,
It smells like a cigarette,
It looks like a jar of red jam,
It sounds like a loud vibration in your head,
It feels like a mouthful of scalding hot food.

Summer Bailey
SS Wulstan's & Edmund's Catholic Primary School & Nursery, Fleetwood

Anger

Anger is like a red, fierce, exploding volcano,
It sounds like a drum pounding in my head,
It looks like a tornado tearing through a town,
It smells like a smelly rat,
It feels like scratching your nails on a cork board,
It tastes like a spicy curry.

Connor Benson (10)
SS Wulstan's & Edmund's Catholic Primary School & Nursery, Fleetwood

Bully

I'm a bully
I bully other children
Maybe I should be nicer
Then I won't get into trouble anymore
There shouldn't be no kicking from me.
I bang on other kids' chairs
But maybe it's annoying
So I'm going to be nice.

Paige Rogers & Lewis Wilson (8)
Sherington Primary School, Charlton

Please Don't

Please don't bully,
It is wrong.
Please don't bully,
Just get along.

Please don't punch,
Please just eat your lunch,
Please don't kick,
Neither pick on people.

Please don't bully,
And don't do
All those things.
Please don't push,
Please don't smack,
And if you do . . .
I'll smack you back.

Rebecca Terry (8)
Sherington Primary School, Charlton

Bullies, Bullies, Bullies

Bullies, bullies, bullies
They try hard to hurt your feelings
Bullies, bullies, bullies
Always there to face.

Bullies are just so painful
They're always there
Just so fierce, no one can stand them.

Bullies, bullies, bullies
They're just too rough
Bullies, bullies, bullies
Watch out, here they come!

China Ryan (9)
Sherington Primary School, Charlton

Bullies

B ullies are bad, mean and sad,
U nkind people you see every day
L ying and stealing, it's all wrong!
L ive your life how you should
Y ou are courageous and cared for
        Don't be scared!

Paris Tomlinson (9)
Sherington Primary School, Charlton

Bullies

I run away from bullies
they frighten me
I am very scared
and when my friends come,
they will help me because
they are my best friends.

I am so scared of bullies,
bullies frighten me
which I don't like.

Bullies make your feelings sad.

Tolu Olamiyam (8)
Sherington Primary School, Charlton

Bullies

B oys and girls always do it,
U sing their feet to trip you up,
L oving to make you cry.
L oving to call out, 'Peanut, what's up?'
I ncidents are what they make,
E ven then they make us cry,
S till they don't know what they're doing is a mistake.

Wilhem J Ngaka (8)
Sherington Primary School, Charlton

Bully

B ullies hurt your feelings
U sing you for everything
L ies are what they tell
L eaving you all alone
Y ou are scared of them.

Cameron Hand (9)
Sherington Primary School, Charlton

Bullies Feel Good

Bullies, bullies are so bad
Bullies, bullies are so proud
Bullies, bullies are not nice
Bullies, bullies call some names
Bullies, bullies push you around
Bullies, bullies rule you around
Bullies, bullies come in a gang
Bullies, bullies feel good
I don't . . .

Grant Biddiss (8)
Sherington Primary School, Charlton

Stop It!

S top it, stop it, it makes us cry
T o all who are hurt, don't be shy.
O pen up your eyes and be kind
P lay together, not against.

I know we can do better
T ogether forever, together we stay.

Chloe Hearnden (8)
Sherington Primary School, Charlton

Bullying

Bullying, bullying
No one likes bullies,
A bully kicks you
A bully pushes you,
A bully pinches you.
It's not very nice to be bullied.
Me and my mates were bullied once.
It's awful to be bullied,
They force you to do something
You don't want to do.
It's awful to be bullied!

Melissa Barden (9)
Sherington Primary School, Charlton

Bullies

Bullies, bullies,
Leave us alone,
You act like the king and queen,
Sitting on a throne.
You call us names,
Tell us what to do,
Why do we have to listen to you?
We've got to speak up,
We're not alone,
We are the ones who deserve the throne.

Tyler Bruiners (8)
Sherington Primary School, Charlton

We Get Over Bullies

Bullying is bad,
It makes people feel sad,
They break people's hearts.
It is not right,
We all hide with fear,
But now I'm going to stick up for myself,
I am not scared anymore!

Ellie Deverill (8)
Sherington Primary School, Charlton

Summer!

S ummer is here
U nder the logs and leaves lie
M ice, hedgehogs, slugs and tiny little flies
M any sunbathe on the lawn
E arwigs drifting asleep at dawn
R oses filling the air with perfume

G olden sun sucking up the cold like a vacuum
A nt colonies racing up the leaves
R ushing bees in and out of the trees
D affodils fading away, like they've just turned edible
E ating caterpillars, soon turn beautiful
N ever-ending fruit that's juicy
S o much dew that's thick and moussey.

Anna Louise Moore (10)
Skelton Newby Hall CE School, Ripon

I Remember

I remember, I remember
Easter morn
The sky changes from black to blue
I stretch and yawn
But now it's just a memory to remember
All night long.

It is Christmas Eve
As me and my brother lay dreamless
Just waiting for the man who is coming
Down the chimney
And I wish that wasn't a memory

It's a winter's day and getting late
The sun drops down, down, down
The snowflakes are melting fast
And that's a winter's poem.

Imogen Hughes (9)
Skelton Newby Hall CE School, Ripon

Things I Like

Things I like and things I do,
Things that really make me chew.
There are really quite a few.
Some old, some new,
There are really quite a few.
Some are good, some are bad.
Some of them make me sad,
Most of them make me glad.
A lot I've never had,
Far too many to mention.

Sophie Dumbreck (9)
Skelton Newby Hall CE School, Ripon

Winter

Winter is a special time when
All the beautiful birds sing and
Where all the children
Are waiting for Christmas.
Christmas is just around
The corner and people are
In the sauna waiting for
Christmas Day.

Jack Sheridan (8) & Thomas Chappell (7)
Skelton Newby Hall CE School, Ripon

My Special Friend

Imagine a person who
Is funny and always
Laughs at your jokes

Imagine a person who
Is kind and helpful
And can keep a secret

Imagine a person who
Sticks up for you
And never leaves you out

Imagine a person who
Is generous and is
Always gentle

Imagine that person
My special friend
Is you.

William Hillson (11)
The Heys Primary School, Ashton-under-Lyne

My Special Friend

Imagine a person who
Looks at your face
And never forgets you in space

Imagine a person who
Laughs when you're funny
And lends you money

Imagine a person who
Plays on his PlayStation 2
And always says 'Boo!'

Imagine a person who
Always loves you
When you're feeling blue

Imagine a person who
Always shares
And plays truth or dare

Imagine a person who
Helps all around
When my body is on the ground

Imagine that person - my special friend - you!

Jaymin Patel (11)
The Heys Primary School, Ashton-under-Lyne

My Special Friend

My special friend is gleeful
She plays nicely all the time.

My special friend is amazing
She tells funny rhymes.

My special friend helps me when
I'm down and she never frowns.

My special friend is always around
My special friend is you!

Nile Pimlott (10)
The Heys Primary School, Ashton-under-Lyne

My Special Friend

Imagine a person
That looks up to you
And respects you

Imagine a person
That cheers you up
When you are down

Imagine a person
That is never alone
Who comforts and cares

Imagine a person
Who you can trust
And share your secrets with

Imagine that person, my special friend, *you!*

Ryan Powell (11)
The Heys Primary School, Ashton-under-Lyne

My Special Friend

Imagine a person,
That looks out for you
When you're down, brings you up.

Imagine a person who
Jumps all around,
Runs, round and round.

Imagine a person who
Is always around you,
Looks out for you.

Imagine a person who
Rules the world,
Is too cool for us.

Callum Cheetham (11)
The Heys Primary School, Ashton-under-Lyne

My Special Friend

Imagine a person who
Is really helpful,
And always comes when you're feeling down.

Imagine a person who's
A funny joker,
And dances like a king.

Imagine a person who
Is polite and encouraging,
And gives you good ideas when you're stuck.

Imagine a person who
Is kind and helpful,
And caring like a star.

Imagine a person who
Is really clever,
And my special friend for ever and ever.

Imagine that person - my special friend,
You!

Jiten Mistry (10)
The Heys Primary School, Ashton-under-Lyne

My Special Friend

My special friend is a . . .
Sloppy kisser,
Game destroyer,
Loveable teddy bear,
Playful puppy,
Gerbil watcher,
Toy chewer,
Food lover,
Lazy sleeper,
Loud barker,
Bird chaser,
Dog hater.

Jack Curry (10)
The Heys Primary School, Ashton-under-Lyne

My Special Friend

Imagine a person who
Likes to play football
Helping you win because you are so tall

Imagine a person who
Likes to play jokes
Because he drinks so much Coke

Imagine a person who
Likes to play the PlayStation
So he encourages us to play

Imagine a person who
Laughs so much
So much that he laughs like a clown

Imagine a person who
Loves to play
Sharing things like games

Imagine a person who
Is kind and friendly
Who likes to share things with other people

Imagine a person who
Is clever and brainy
Who helps other people with his ideas

Imagine a person who
Looks out for you
Who cares for the family he loves and the friends he's got

Imagine a person who is my special friend - you.

Bhavin Mistry (10)
The Heys Primary School, Ashton-under-Lyne

My Special Friend

Imagine a person who
Makes you happy when you're down
Cares for you when you're around

Imagine a person who
Brings a smile to your face
Makes you happy in any place

Imagine a person who
Sticks up for you
You'll always have someone to talk to

Imagine a person who
Likes to sing and dance
Goes around and has a glance

Imagine that person, my special friend - *you!*

Sarah Greenwood (10)
The Heys Primary School, Ashton-under-Lyne

My Special Friend

Imagine a person sweet and kind and
makes your mind as good as mine.

Imagine a person so funny and loud
and never lets you down.

Imagine a person who looks out for you
when you're hurt and you're being bullied.

Imagine a person who helps you with
your homework and work.

Imagine a best friend like *you!*

Lauren Richardson (10)
The Heys Primary School, Ashton-under-Lyne

My Special Friend

Imagine a person who
Is very caring
And is also very daring.

Imagine a person who
Tackles your dreads
And always keeps a cool head.

Imagine a person who
Lightens you up
And also can tell when you're down in the dumps.

Imagine a person who
Is very kind
And when they're upset, speak their mind.

Imagine that person - my special friend - *you!*

Meera Mistry (11)
The Heys Primary School, Ashton-under-Lyne

My Special Friend

Imagine a person who
Would help me up when I am hurt

Imagine a person who
Would play with me when I am alone

Imagine a person who
Takes me to shelter when it's raining

Imagine a person who
Would help me when I'm trapped
Like the little girl in the hole.

Leon Moreton (10)
The Heys Primary School, Ashton-under-Lyne

My Special Friend

Imagine a friend who
Loves you and cares for you
Chases your feet up the stairs.

Imagine a friend who
Lets you tickle his belly
Curls up next to you when you're down.

Imagine a friend who
Plays with you when you're blue
Cries when he's hungry.

Imagine a friend who
Tells you when to leave him alone
Is cute, wise and makes you laugh!

Imagine that friend, my special friend - *you!*

Bernadette Nolan (10)
The Heys Primary School, Ashton-under-Lyne

My Special Friend

Imagine a person who
Is very kind
And has got his own mind.

Imagine a person who
Is very tall
Will not fall

Imagine a person who
Is very good
And is very good luck

Imagine a person who
Will be good to you.

James Davison (10)
The Heys Primary School, Ashton-under-Lyne

My Special Friend

Imagine a person who
Plays football
Just like you.

Imagine a person
With sticky-up hair
Like a hedgehog

Imagine a person
Who looks up
To you

Imagine a person who
Sits all on his own
In a classroom

Imagine a person
It is everyone
My friend, my friend.

Colin Clifford (10)
The Heys Primary School, Ashton-under-Lyne

My Special Friend

Imagine a person
Who helps you when you're down,
Who never wears a frown.

Imagine a person
Who is a guru at games,
Who goes with his dream.

Imagine a person,
Who keeps a friendship,
Likes a little joke
Imagine that person - my special friend, you.

Daniel Eades (10)
The Heys Primary School, Ashton-under-Lyne

A Superhero Sends A Letter Home

Dear Mum,
      I'm still not good,
Send some food if you could,
The stains still won't come out,
And Ali Tosis gave me a clout,
I had a fight, guess what? I lost,
I don't like to take the cost,
When fighting with Ali you need a nose peg,
In the end I had a broken leg,
So as you see I'm not the best,
So I had better have a rest,
Next time I write I should be better,
So now I shall end my letter,
Your loving daughter,
A failing hero.

Emily Wilson (11)
Uplands CP School, Stroud

A Superhero Sends A Letter Home

Dear Mum,
      I am great.
Had a fight with someone I hate.
Nearly killed me, she did.
Trying to fight with another kid.
Stealing money she was again.
Man, she put me through pain.
Climbing buildings all year round.
I nearly fell right to the ground.
Caught her though with a pow.
Everyone clapped and I took a bow.
Got to go, in a rush,
There's loads to do and time's at a push.
I'll write soon, cheerio.
Your loving daughter, a failing hero.

Jessica Vines (10)
Uplands CP School, Stroud

A Superhero Sends A Letter Home

Dear Mum,
    I am fine.
I hope you haven't been drinking too much wine!
Ali Tosis is going well.
Despite the fact of his bad breath smell.
Me and Ali had a fight.
He screamed at me with all his might.
But we made up and are fine now.
Is it going to last? I don't know how.
My powers are getting low.
Even though it's hard to show.
I think my brains are going to pot.
But not as bad as Bogieman's snot!
I really hope I see you soon
Because you sparkle like the moon.
Got to go, see you later!
Your loving daughter
A failing hero.

Jennifer West (10)
Uplands CP School, Stroud

List Poem

An angry, fierce pineapple exploded
while getting her spotty scarlet dress on.
The lonely, spotty emerald moon
sang peacefully like a hummingbird.
The jolly, happy blossom giggled really loudly
because he fell gently on the floor.
The slender balloon flew as high as he could.
The two talking chairs chattered as they walked by.
The rough snake slithered along the long, blowy grass.
Slyly, the huge, slimy, green and yellow slug
was crawling along the concrete ground.

Jade Mather (8)
Uplands CP School, Stroud

A Superhero To A Super Zero

Dear Dad,
My life is quite bad,
It all started with a Twix,
Inside was a poison mix.
The wrinkly ninja helped,
But when he touched me I yelped.
I banged my head yesterday,
I landed in a stack of hay.
A cow chased me round and round,
I landed in a cowpat mound.
Oh please let me come home
And please get me some bath foam.
Hope to see you later,
Alligator.

Russell Gardiner (9)
Uplands CP School, Stroud

A Superhero Sends A Letter Home

Dear Mum,
Something's wrong with my weather powers,
I can't stop the April showers.
My career as a superhero is turning into
a big fat zero.
My gigantic fire supernova
has destroyed my pretty, love life Clover.
Oh please let me come back home,
I need some medicine for my big ear syndrome.
Heat vision not bad at all,
until I found out I'd destroyed the town hall.
I'm sorry I feel so bad,
but I still love you though.
From your lovely lad,
                        Chad.

Georgie H Clifford (11)
Uplands CP School, Stroud

A Superhero Sends A Letter Home

Dear Mum,
I feel great,
But not as good as Jason Clate.
My healing powers are going down the drain,
Just the same as all the rain.
My super strength has gone low,
Even though it's hard to show.
The coffee stains,
Are somehow giving me pains.
My tights are itchy,
They're shrinking, titchy.
But now I'm better
And the rain's got wetter.
I wear a bow,
From Bow Bow and Co.
Well, got to go now,
So I'll take a bow.
From your not so superhero daughter.

Jessica Francis (11)
Uplands CP School, Stroud

Seaside

Happiness
Happiness is making slimy, slippery sandcastles.
Happiness is bodyboarding on the huge waves.
Happiness is paddling in the shiny, salty sea.
Happiness is a lush chocolate chip ice cream melting in your hands.

Sadness
Sadness is when you can't get away from jellyfish.
Sadness is swallowing smelly saltwater.
Sadness is getting wet and sand sticking to you and making you itchy.
Sadness is being lost on a crowded beach.

Amelia Parnell (8)
Uplands CP School, Stroud

Seaside Poem

Happiness
Happiness is going crab catching in the freezing cold sea.
Happiness is riding big, friendly, brown donkeys.
Happiness is paddling with Pepper the dog in the wavy sea,
$\qquad\qquad\qquad\qquad\qquad$ shining like glitter.
Happiness is collecting tiny, smooth fish.
Happiness is having a chocolate ice cream with a chocolate flake.
Happiness is sunbathing in the scorching sun.

Eloise Humpheys (8)
Uplands CP School, Stroud

Fun Poem

The angry pin burst the girl's balloon!
The blue grass danced happily through the night
The tall grass danced in the wind
The smooth sword glittered like a star.

Daniel Bateman (7)
Uplands CP School, Stroud

Sea Feeling

Happiness
Happiness is running away from the swishy sea.
Happiness is going on smiling donkeys.
Happiness is lying in the shiny sun.
Happiness is paddling in the smooth, deep blue sea.
Happiness is making sloppy brown sandcastles.
Happiness is having lovely hot fish and chips.
Happiness is collecting shiny seashells.

Kimberley Legge (8)
Uplands CP School, Stroud

Autumn

The leaves fall off the trees like a gliding hummingbird.
The leaves crunch as loud as a dinosaur stamping.
The prickly hedgehogs snuggle up tightly like a tiger cub.
The beautiful brown squirrels collect crunchy nuts for winter.
The deer eat their food like a quiet mouse hunting cheese!

Jenna Mather (8) & Marc Hudson (7)
Uplands CP School, Stroud

Seaside Poems

Happiness is when the wet, warm sea washes on your tingling toes.
Happiness is eating a cold creamy ice cream.
Happiness is soggy salty fish and chips.
Happiness is looking in the shady rock pools for bright-red crabs.
Happiness is digging a huge, wet, shelly hole.
Happiness is sunbathing in the boiling hot sunshine.

Sadness is when you get burnt by the boiling hot sun.
Sadness is when you have just been pushed into the sea.
Sadness is when you sink into the dark blue ocean.
Sadness is when you fall off your bodyboard.
Sadness is when you've just been bitten by a bright red crab.

Sarah Locke (7)
Uplands CP School, Stroud

Autumn

Leaves as red as fire scattering onto the ground like icing on a cake.
Leaves tumble off the trees leaving them bare, swirling, twirling down!
Squirrels collect nuts for the long cold winter.
Longer, spookier, darker nights.
Starving deer chomp on damp bark.
Hedgehogs hibernate, getting ready for cold winter days.

Harriet Dee (8)
Uplands CP School, Stroud

Autumn

Autumn is leaves falling off the trees, different colours like a dolly mix.
Autumn is animals hibernating and keeping warm in their den.
Autumn is furry squirrels collecting nuts.
Autumn is starving deer eating cold bark off the trees.
Autumn is nights getting longer and days getting darker.
Autumn is windy and stormy and rainy days.
Autumn is when the birds twitter and chatter all day.
Autumn is when leaves crunch like crisps.
Autumn is when ducks and swans bite your toes.

Amy Allard (8) & Charlie Tocknell (7)
Uplands CP School, Stroud

Autumn

Autumn, autumn, leaves fall off like a tapping drum.
Autumn, autumn, leaves blow away like a gust of wind.
Autumn, autumn, the leaves are as red as strawberry jelly.
Autumn, autumn, the grass is covered in frost.
Autumn, autumn, leaves rustle like animals hiding in the trees.

Naomi Chandler (8) & James Bathe (7)
Uplands CP School, Stroud

Autumn

Brown baby deer crunching bark.
Cheeky pipsqueak squirrels collecting brown nuts.
Animals hibernating in warm burrows and dark trees.
Night growing darker and the stars shining as bright as fireflies.
Dark, cold, damp, windy nights.
Grass swaying like a magnificent ballet dancer.
Brown, orange and red leaves flying down like a blue tit.
Leaves swooping down like an eagle hunting for his prey.
Crunch, crunch, leaves shattering on the floor.
Brown spiky hedgehogs snuggle up in their dens.
Brown bears sleeping in their caves.

Suzanna Ward (9) & Georgia Harris (8)
Uplands CP School, Stroud

Autumn

Leaves as red as fire, drift off a tree.
Rabbits hibernate into their deep burrows.
An unhealthy deer chomps on wet bark like a wood chopper
                                chopping down a thin tree.
Small squirrels gather their rock-solid nuts.
Trees as brown as wholemeal bread tumble down.
Finally autumn ends.

James Rees (9)
Uplands CP School, Stroud

Autumn

Leaves falling off the trees like a bird swooping through the sky.
Animals hibernating in their warm cosy homes.
Squirrels collecting nuts so they don't starve during the freezing winter.
Deer eating dark bark.
Wet, juicy, bright green grass sways like classic dancers on stage.
Children splashing in the wet, warm puddles.
The sound of children standing on crunchy brown leaves sounds like
                                crunchy chocolate bars.
The sound of robins chirping their highest notes like singers
                                singing lovely songs.

Ryan Burrage (8)
Uplands CP School, Stroud

Autumn

The crispy, crunchy leaves flutter down from the big bare tree.
Hedgehogs hibernate in their snuggly hole.
The nights increase like an elastic band.
When people walk, the leaves whisper with glee.
Squirrels collect massive, round, juicy nuts for winter.
The rain comes down like bombs from the sky.
Deer chew tasty bark off the giant trees.

Oscar Riordan (8) & Daniel Bateman (7)
Uplands CP School, Stroud

Autumn

Leaves falling off the branches, orange, yellow, red and brown.
The wind blowing through the trees like a huge, fierce hurricane.
Deer crunching on dark thick bark.
Squirrels collecting juicy nuts and curling up in their warm homes.
The grass swaying in the icy breeze.
The foxes howling in the dark, dark night.

Bryannie Konya (7) & Cameron Griffiths (8)
Uplands CP School, Stroud

Autumn

The crunchy leaves float in the air.
The grey squirrels scatter through the long wavy grass.
The badgers hibernate in the dark soft soil.
The nights turn darker and longer.
The delicious blackberries ready to put on a pie.
The rushing bird going home, whizzing through the air like a racing car.

Laura Chandler (8) & Bradley Barrow (7)
Uplands CP School, Stroud

Dogs

Food eater
Good sleeper
Barking mad
Very bad
Face licker
Bone hider
Tail wagger
Friends forever.

Melissa Blundell (9)
Wilburton VPC School, Ely

Rain

When it rains,
It's really cool.
The rain goes spit, spat
Getting wetter . . .
Wetter.
The child is watching,
She can't go out and play.

It's cold and shivery.
Raincoats, hats and scarves.
Bored and unhappy
Playing games.
Inside and cosy
Snuggled warm.
Watching . . .
And waiting
Till it stops.

Bethany Flack (10)
Wilburton VPC School, Ely

Birds

Fantastic flyer
Worm pecker
Wing waver
Skydiver
Cloud skipper
Skyscraper
Bug eater
Non digger
Sometimes swimmer
Ground hopper.

Freddie Upton (9)
Wilburton VPC School, Ely

Anger

Anger is red like a fire when it's flaring
Anger is a cauldron bubbling over
Anger feels like you are struck by lightning
Anger is a hurricane that no one can survive
Anger smells like the smoke of a forest fire
Anger tastes like a red-hot spicy pepper that no one can eat
Anger reminds me of a volcano erupting.

Jenny Weldon (11)
Wilburton VPC School, Ely

Love

Love is pink like a beautiful flower.
It is like a harp being plucked in a billowing cloud.
Love feels like it's snowing on Christmas Day.
Love looks like two doves flying in the beautiful sky.
Love smells like a bunch of blossoms.
Love tastes like cherry lipstick.
Love reminds me of my first date.

Joshua Robinson (10)
Wilburton VPC School, Ely

Sadness

Sadness is blue like the gushing sea,
It is the sound no one can hear like everlasting silence,
It feels like I'll never know what happiness is,
It looks like I'm the only one,
It smells so empty that no one can smell anything,
It tastes like tears from my eye,
It reminds me of all the sad times I've had.

Anjela Griffiths (11)
Wilburton VPC School, Ely

Love

Love is pink like a rose
Settling on the ground.
Whistling in the air,
Sounding nice and gentle.
Snowing on Christmas Eve.
Snow falling from the sky.
The smell of cherries falling.
It tastes like cherry pie.
It reminds me of my mum.

Christopher Coe (9)
Wilburton VPC School, Ely

Anger

Red is like anger.
Anger is adrenalin rushing through my veins.
Anger sounds like a beating drum in my ear.
Anger feels like you need to hit someone to make it stop.
It looks like a fire that never burns out.
It smells like smoke from burning coal.
Anger tastes like a rotting body.
Anger reminds me of people being shot and killed.

Harley Pyne (10)
Wilburton VPC School, Ely

Anger

Anger is red like a volcano ready to explode
Anger is loud like the stamping of feet
Anger makes me feel like running away
Anger looks like a roof blowing off a house
Anger smells like a hot burning fire
Anger tastes like hot, spicy crisps
Anger reminds me of a killing toothache.

Abigail Weldon (9)
Wilburton VPC School, Ely

Funfair

Colourful lighting
Swirling drums
Bumpy ski jump
Bouncy castle
Jumping frog
Shooting bungee jump
Bumping dodgems
Galloping gallopers
Corks shooting.

Jade Harris (9)
Wilburton VPC School, Ely

The Snail

Trail maker
Floor slider
Home carrier
Wall climber
Leaf muncher
Bird fodder
Garden pesterer.

Philip Kirby (10)
Wilburton VPC School, Ely

Happiness

Happiness is the colour blue like the plain sky.
Happiness is a sweet whistle in my head.
Happiness feels like a cloud.
Happiness looks like a twinkle in the sky.
Happiness smells like the sea.
Happiness tastes like a warm piece of bread.
Happiness reminds me of my first day of school.

Brook Line (9)
Wilburton VPC School, Ely

Fear

Fear is black,
Like a pitch-black night.
Fear is a scream,
Crashing through the night.
Fear is,
A white, hot dagger in your chest.
Fear looks like,
A vampire running past a grave.
Fear smells like
A house burning in the night.
Fear tastes like
Blood in your water.
Fear reminds you,
Of the first time you got lost.

Austin Line (10)
Wilburton VPC School, Ely

Anger

Anger harmful
Tasty spiteful
Always there
Never bare
Disobeying
Always paying
Nasty words
Charging herds
Making sad
Very bad
Knocking things
Taking rings.

Josh Greene (10)
Wilburton VPC School, Ely

Sadness

Sadness is a blue tear from an angel in the sky.
It sounds like the waves splashing on an empty sea.
It feels like you are lost with nowhere to go.
It looks like a fairy losing its wings.
It smells like a flower starting to die.
It tastes like something that will never go away.
It reminds me of a friend starting to cry.

Katie Easton (10)
Wilburton VPC School, Ely

The Pigs

The pigs are killed
For their bodies
The people feel sorry
For all the things
They did to the pigs
But they still eat
Sausages, chops and bacon
Night and day
The people are well fed
But the pigs are dead!

Ryan Dodd (10)
Wilburton VPC School, Ely

Darkness

Darkness is black like the midnight sky.
Darkness is the sound of the cackling Devil.
Darkness is the time of the haunting hours.
It looks like the lair of all things evil.
It smells of the burning flesh of the Devil.
It tastes like the trickling blood of a vampire.
It reminds me of all things evil and dead.

Ross Payne (10)
Wilburton VPC School, Ely

Sadness

Sadness is like blue
Like an everlasting rainfall
Sadness sounds like silence
That will never be disturbed
It feels like happiness
Will never come my way
It looks like I'm the only one
That is sad
Sadness smells like the emptiness
Of an empty room
It tastes like salt from a tear
It reminds me of all the bad things
That have happened to me.

Mellissa Binks (10)
Wilburton VPC School, Ely

Food And You

I like sweets
And sugary treats
But mostly I like you
Pineapples and apples
I don't go to a chapel
I think most cows go moo.

Down in the cellar
I think your name is Bella
You are really cool
I want some food
My friend is in a mood
You are in the pool.

Anna Fletcher (10)
Ysgol Cynfran, Colwyn Bay

Untitled

There was a ghost, a really terrifying ghost,
Who sucked out people's souls.
His name was Scary,
But everyone called him Scream.
'The Scream' his name was,
Everyone hid and screamed at the terrifying Scream,
He was the most shocking of them all.

He came again and again,
To kill, but he couldn't.
Everyone had gone.
They knew he would be back,
He stayed until they came back
And made them scream again.
He found out where they were and screamed again,
All would dread to see him again.

Brian Williams (10)
Ysgol Cynfran, Colwyn Bay

Listening

Listening helps you learn
Listening helps you read
Listening helps you do your work
Listening helps you do your language
Listening helps you do your maths homework.

Listening helps you become smart
Listening helps you spell people's names
Listening helps you work
Listening helps you read a good or bad book
Listening helps you be good.

Immogen Steward (9)
Ysgol Cynfran, Colwyn Bay

Moon

I would love to sit on the moon,
The moon is shaped like the top of a spoon.
I would sit on the moon,
I would think of my room,
I would sit there till the afternoon.

I would like to see the moon,
I would like to see it very soon,
I would like to take a balloon with me,
I would take a really big flask of tea.

I would like to see the moon in a rocket,
I would hate anything to come out of a socket.
I would sit there thinking,
I am shrinking.

Jemma Roberts (9)
Ysgol Cynfran, Colwyn Bay

Football

In football we wear long pants,
In football we squash ants.
In football we kick the ball
At the wall.
We play football on a hill
With Jack and Jill.

In football we have boys,
That still like toys,
In football we have girls,
That like to eat Twirls.
In football we have a dog
That sits quietly on a log.

Jessica Foster (9)
Ysgol Cynfran, Colwyn Bay

My Cat

My cat is nice and gentle, furry ginger
Black and white. She curls, she swirls,
She purrs on me, she sleeps with me
Now you know what my cat is like
My cat runs up and down the stairs,
Around the house, she slips on the floor.
She runs next door,
She drinks milk, she eats nearly everything.

Sam Faux (9)
Ysgol Cynfran, Colwyn Bay

Birthdays

Balloons and treats
And sugary sweets
Blushing with yellow and red
Party bags filled with joy
Music flowing over your head
Last and least of all, the feast
Is cakes with candles on top
Happy Birthday!

Ashleigh Jordan Howard
Ysgol Cynfran, Colwyn Bay

The Stars

The stars are shiny
The stars are bright
They are huge
They are small in the night
I like the stars they are great.
They are like my mates
I think I could be a star
Because I like stars
I can see them in the car.

Dillon James Faux (9)
Ysgol Cynfran, Colwyn Bay

Winter

Winter is very cold
Winter is very bold.
If you like the winter chill
You'll be in for a thrill.

Winter has a cold breeze
Winter makes all ponds freeze
If you're in a race, you won't go fast
You'll just end up last.

Winter has a load of frost
Winter makes the ground lost.
At winter, we enjoy the birth of Christ
The snow in winter is as white as mice.

Caen Warren (10)
Ysgol Cynfran, Colwyn Bay

Chester Zoo

Yesterday, we went to Chester Zoo,
There were so many animals
And lots and lots to do.

We rode on the monorail, up so high.
We saw so many animals from our view point
Up so high.

We went to see the sea lions,
The monkeys too.
So many animals and lots and lots to do.

We went to the park,
We stayed there till dark.
I went on the swings
They were shaped like rings.

India Hughes (9)
Ysgol Cynfran, Colwyn Bay

My Lucky Hamster

My lucky hamster jumps in my hands
My lucky hamster runs around wild.
My lucky hamster bites my mum's ear,
My lucky hamster hides in the bin.
My lucky hamster acts like a bat.
My lucky hamster jumps around crazy,
My lucky hamster out runs a cat.
My lucky hamster acts like it's dead.
My lucky hamster plays with my dog.
My lucky hamster's name's Lucky.

Rhys Rowlings
Ysgol Cynfran, Colwyn Bay

I Like To Be Both

I like to be naughty
I don't like to be good
I like to be both, instead of good.

If you are naughty
You are cool
If you are good
You get praised
So I think I will be good for the rest of my days.

Leila Parker (9)
Ysgol Cynfran, Colwyn Bay

Close Encounters

Here is the maze
Here is where you enter
Here is the path that leads to the centre

Here are the bones of those who have tried
To find a way out
But failed and died.

Susan avoided the cracks with great care
And always trod upon the square
An unwise move she was to discover
She stepped on a manhole without a cover.

Here lies the body of little Jack Horner
Ate too much Christmas pie
And dropped dead in his corner.

Here lies the body of Fast Eddy Jakes
Invented a sports car without any brakes.

Here lies the body of Tracey Plumb
Sucked her body away, began with her thumb.

He passed the bobby without any fuss
He passed the cart of hay
He tried to pass a swerving bus
And then he passed away.

John Mark Gill (9)
Ysgol Cynfran, Colwyn Bay